EVEN *the* WIND

MATT FOSTER ~ MICHELLE LEWIS ~ AXEL LIIMATTA

All Scripture quotations, unless otherwise indicated, are taken from the Holy Bible, New International Version®, NIV®.

Copyright ©1973, 1978, 1984, 2011 by Biblica, Inc.™ Used by permission of Zondervan.

All rights reserved worldwide.
www.zondervan.com

The "NIV" and "New International Version" are trademarks registered in the United States Patent and Trademark Office by Biblica, Inc.™

Copyright © 2021 by Whetstone Boys Ranch

All rights reserved. No part of this book may be reproduced or used in any manner without written permission of the copyright owner except for the use of quotations in a book review. For more information, address: aliimatta@whetstoneboysranch.com

First paperback edition September 2021
Independently Published

Book design by Amanda Howerton Design

ISBN 979-8-4645-4801-5 (paperback)

Whetstone Boys Ranch
6850 County Road 2660
Mountain View, MO 65548
417-934-1112

> The men were amazed and asked, "What kind of man is this? Even the winds and the waves obey him!"
>
> *Matthew 8:27*

TO THE BOYS OF WHETSTONE:

> May you come to see
> that who you are
> is not at war
> with who your loving Father
> created you to be.
>
> And may you be
> truly happy...
>
> wherever by the wind
> you may be carried.

Table of Contents

Acknowledgements vii
Editor's Note ix
Foreword xi

Calm: Foxes Have Dens

1. Weather Radio 15
2. Terra Incognita 19
3. April Fools 23

Call: Follow Me

4. Flowmaster 31
5. Corn Dogs 33
6. Space Helmets 37

Chaos: Lord, Save Us!

7. Alert 45
8. Chainsaws 49
9. Covers 55
10. Small 59
11. Donuts 61

Control: Why Are You So Afraid?

12. Fallen 69
13. Glass House 71
14. Imagery 75
15. Tarps 79
16. Empty 85
17. In the Dark 87

18. Salvage — 91
19. Garden Variety — 95
20. Aroma — 97
21. Incrementalism — 101
22. Horses — 103
23. Stu — 107
24. Big Boy — 111
25. Buried Alive — 117
26. Country Roads — 119

COMFORT: WHAT KIND OF MAN IS THIS?

27. Proof — 125
28. Yeast — 129
29. Forks, pt.1 — 133
30. Spot — 137
31. False Hope — 139
32. Forks, pt.2 — 141
33. Sylvia Plath — 143
34. The Dark Knight — 147
35. Pigs — 151
36. Dictionary — 153
37. Reframe — 157
38. Spent — 161
39. Casablanca — 165
40. You Do You — 171
41. #YouToo — 173
42. Caves — 175
43. Tomorrow — 181
44. Christmas — 183
45. TIME — 187
46. Dry Bones — 191
47. Slide Show — 195
48. Yellow — 197
49. Snapshot — 201

About the Authors — 204

Acknowledgements

The authors of this book would like to extend their deepest felt thanks to the following people:

Our spouses, first and foremost—fellow laborers in a field not always white unto harvest but into which we are called to gather what God has made to grow.

Our children, whose patience, understanding, and support of our work is an absolute prerequisite. You are precious beyond all words.

Jeremy Thompson, executive director at Whetstone, who has graciously made allowances of time and money to make this happen. This is a book, if ever there was one, written in the tight spaces of living.

Dave Malone, special agent of all things literary, whose timely advice and sincere enthusiasm for this project is most responsible for its final shape and form.

The many enthusiastic readers who took time to offer their honest opinions of this manuscript in its various forms. This book will be more helpful to others because of their encouragement and honesty.

The community of stakeholders in and around Mountain View, Missouri, whose love, trust, and support has made us feel truly welcome in these Ozark Hills.

Former house parents, teachers, mentoring specialists, interns, and all other direct-care staff who have made and continue to make Whetstone a place where families are sharpened and futures are shaped.

The thousands of donors, volunteers, and prayer warriors all across this country and globe, whose mustard seed faith in us has made all the difference.

And lastly, the parents, grandparents, aunts, uncles, siblings, guardians, and caregivers who have entrusted us with life's most precious gift—a child. We are most grateful for this trust, and we pray that this book honors your commitment to him and to the great sacrifices you have made to get him back.

Editor's Note

Axel

This story is told mainly from three different perspectives:

- ~ Matt Foster—primary therapist and program director at Whetstone Boys Ranch.
- ~ Michelle Lewis—house mom at Whetstone Boys Ranch.
- ~ Axel Liimatta—headmaster of Whetstone Academy, the therapeutic boarding school that all residents attend.

Beyond this, a handful of sections are told from two other perspectives:

- ~ Joey Padovano—mentoring specialist who lived at the ranch during the time of the tornado.
- ~ Whetstone Residents—boys, ages 13–16, who survived a terrifying ordeal and who will remain anonymous for reasons of privacy. They are often referred to in this text as the "Whetstone boys," to distinguish them from Michelle's boys, and they are identified by the use of a single capital letter, such as K—, or P—.

Switches in perspective are indicated by the name placed beneath or beside the title of the chapter. Great effort has been spent to keep the narrative as linear as possible; but if at times readers find themselves swirling around a bit—well, perhaps that's how it should be in a book about life's tornadoes.

Foreword

On April 6, 2015, I cashed a check at Community First Bank in West Plains, Missouri. The teller clicked at her computer keys and asked me how long it would be before Whetstone Boys Ranch would reopen.

I must have looked bewildered.

"Oh, you haven't heard about the tornado," she said. She swiftly pulled up pictures of the devastation on her computer and turned the screen toward me. I gasped.

As a part-time worker and resident clergy at the ranch, I had an erratic schedule. Slated to work that very afternoon, I exited the bank uncertain what to do.

Several attempts to reach the ranch by phone proved futile, but I quickly learned from others that the extent of the damage would definitely mean a night off. In the paper the next day, a reporter quoted Whetstone's executive director, Jeremy Thompson, who said it would be two to three months before the ranch reopened for business.

In the meantime, the residents would either go to another facility or back home. Clean-up efforts and renovation work would begin immediately.

This was April. It wasn't until Christmas that I was called to resume my work at the ranch.

By the time I returned, the physical restoration was almost complete. There were, of course, telltale signs of the disaster: once-proud trees were gone, and so were three of the outbuildings. Inside the main facility, diligent workers had crafted structural modifications and improvements. Only one of the boys I had worked with the previous spring was still enrolled.

Such devastation can neither be foreseen nor fully comprehended, and the question "Why?" is certain to arise. But the faithful don't linger here. They try to learn and carry on.

And this is precisely what Whetstone has done. They are still standing because of their refusal to stand still.

That being said, the philosopher and theologian inside of me prompt a modest proposal, if not an answer.

The world in which we live is, in itself, a rather drab, gray place. Storm clouds loom. The cold, hard reality is that there are no sounds or colors in the outside world—only waves of various lengths. It is only as these waves are received and processed by our ears and eyes that they are transformed into the beautiful sounds and tinctures that we so admire.

In a similar fashion, God sees things our eyes cannot behold. It is only through His eyes that we can eventually make sense of such events as the tornado that devastated the ranch. All we can do in the meantime is to learn from and be thankful for the trial—no matter how daunting it might seem in the present moment.

Mike Heston
Minister, Ret.
M.A. (Theology and Philosophy)
Lincoln Christian University
Author of *Theology at the Water Street Lounge*

CALM

"Foxes Have Dens..."

Foxes have dens and birds have nests, but the
Son of Man has no place to lay his head.

MATTHEW 8:20

Chapter 1

Weather Radio

Michelle

"We all sleep upstairs in this house," I said to my husband as we peeled back our covers. "That means if a tornado comes, we're all dead," I continued, suddenly concerned for our own three boys and the five Whetstone boys living with us.

Ty crawled into bed. He's a tall cowboy type, and he shuffled around trying to get comfortable, with his long legs and all.

"Yeah," he said, not really paying attention from what I could tell. He put his head down on the pillow but faced me, his eyes dark and sleepy but open.

He had just clocked out on the other side of our dual universe.

You see, we're the house parents at Whetstone Boys Ranch—where the phrase "Honey, I'll be a little late this evening," means "I have to comfort a homesick teenage boy, life coach a twenty-year-old intern, and then write up my daily report before crossing over to our slice of a 10,000 square foot facility in order to kiss our own sleeping boys goodnight."

Midnight loomed.

"I'm worried," I continued, not taking the hint from Ty's silence. "We live out here miles from the city limits. None of us would hear the sirens. How would we even know if a tornado were coming? Just out of the pitch black—wham, dead. We're dead. We'd all be dead."

"Yep," he murmured, with his eyes closed.

I'm pretty sure he was almost asleep by then, my voice like a comforting bedtime story, lulling my husband to sleep.

Our bedroom is far enough from the boys' side that I can't hear them snore. But I often think of them over there, sawing logs. I pray for them to sleep well and to have sweet dreams even though I know this doesn't happen often. They are fretful sleepers, Thomas tells me. Thomas is our night staff who sits in the hall all night long and checks on the boys every fifteen minutes. He's a big guy, and he has to duck under the door frame if he enters a room.

He does a good job of making sure they are all safe, but he can't do anything to stop J—'s court appointment next week. The judge will decide what consequences he gets for lighting a trashcan fire in a school back home. J—'s a nice kid, but he doesn't usually think his actions all the way through.

I see this a lot in the boys who live with us. They seem like they're stuck in the present moment, afraid to look back or to look ahead.

Living in the moment seems like a good philosophy until suddenly it isn't.

I lay in bed that night, worrying about the ranch boys. Worrying about *our* boys. I thought about how we needed a plan if a storm should come.

Ty snored.

A couple weeks later, my thoughtful husband brought home a few weather radios—one for the ranch and one for us. Apparently, he had been listening to me after all.

I am a soccer mom. Literally. I'm a mom who played soccer all the way through college. I was pretty good, and I pride myself in my athleticism, taking the opportunity when it presents itself to dribble through surprised boys who haven't the faintest clue about how to play defense. I usually miss the goal on purpose . . . after weaving through them without breaking a sweat. Teenage boys have fragile egos.

Along with my athletic build, I stand at 5'5", about seven inches shorter than my husband. I have slightly wavy, nut-brown hair that usually comes to my shoulders. On Saturday nights, this hair is usually tied back since the weekends are work shifts for me and my family—although weekends are about as close as some ranch boys can get to normal and relaxing family time.

Their biological families are spread out across the country—from California to New Jersey, and from Michigan to Texas. These young men sometimes spend up to a year with us, so even though they sometimes object to terms like "*home*work" and "*family* night," they can't escape the notion that we are all, at the very least, a domestic unit in some practical sense.

The problem is that for these boys, family means tension. A quiet evening at home around the fire, playing board games, and sipping hot cocoa is a thing in the long forgotten past or a thing that never existed. In its place are screaming, door-slamming, and window-smashing. In extreme cases, this has become the way that they connect. They literally have no knowledge of how to do relationship. Everything they know is wrong, but they can't stop doing it.

Of course, I didn't know this when I signed up to be a house parent. I thought a few cookies and a warm fire would go a lot farther than they actually do.

One Saturday night, not long after we had set up the weather radios, a scary looking stormfront approached from our south. From the big glass windows that surround the living room on the ground floor, we all watched the storm as it gathered strength. We gathered around the radio and listened to its path through Howell and the surrounding counties.

B—, a fifteen-year-old who had been in and out of group homes for the last two years, held the radio up on his shoulder like a boom box and hauled it around our circle of couches and chairs. He was overweight, and his belly kind of bounced around in his loose-fitting sweatshirt. We chuckled at his antics.

"Pull up your pants," Ty said, wanting to save him a bit of embarrassment, should the elastic waistband not be up to the task.

Knowing we might end up under a tornado watch that evening, Ty reminded the boys at dinner about the tornado policy and emergency plans. He instructed them where to go, what to do, and who to follow. We deemed the ping pong room in the basement as our safe room.

"You guys got it? You understand?" he pressed.

"Yeah, yeah," they all chimed.

As they moved upstairs to get ready for bed, I overheard their chatter.

"I wish a tornado would hit Whetstone," one of them said.

Chapter 2

Terra Incognita

Matt

This is the end. The end of K—'s residence at Whetstone Boys Ranch. He wears a nice fitting pair of Wrangler jeans, along with a neatly tucked snap-button shirt, leather belt, and Justin boots shined just for the occasion. He looks good. He looks . . . ready.

He's come a long way from the boy who locked himself in his parents' car on the first day and refused to come out, banging and thrashing on the console. It took several hours of coaxing to get him out and his parents back in. This evening he'll be on the road to Nebraska—which by the way, you can't get to from here.

"I know *so* much more than you guys," he told one staff member on his first day, rolling his eyes and heaving a world-weary sigh that still hangs in the driveway one year later.

As the program director and therapist, I rarely sit during a boy's graduation ceremony. I'm too worked up. And this day is no exception.

Typically, I stand in the back, all five feet and nine inches of my sturdy figure hidden in the adjoining kitchen shadows, where I peer out from behind stylish glasses and a neatly trimmed goatee. Some might say I'm here because I get a jump start on the tasty snacks which follow, and they would not be wrong. But it also gives me a great opportunity to look over the whole crowd celebrating this special day.

An eclectic mix has gathered on this occasion for K—, one month before the tornado. There are the obligatory invitees—the staff, other residents, and immediate family. There are doctors, clergy, volunteers, board members, and beneficiaries of this boys' community service. All have crammed into the tiny living room and onto every piece of furniture we can justify sitting on . . . and some that we can't.

It's a special event, as it should be. K— has worked hard for twelve months, and he has earned a bona fide celebration.

The occasion demands that I draw from my deep well of Latin phrases and deliver one perfectly suited for this boy and his family during a short speech. It's a Matt Foster tradition. Other staff have their graduation thing—vintage vinyl, art work, poetry, and live music, to name a few. I'm the Latin-phrase guy.

The routine axioms I am prone to using during counseling sessions aren't going to cut it today. I've already covered *quid pro quo, tabula rasa*, and *post hoc ergo propter hoc . . . ad nauseum*.

This must be more. It must be a profound utterance from one of the ancients, reaching out to us from across the centuries. No pressure.

Having carefully written it on a 3x5 card that fits neatly in the palm of my hand, I will soon move to the front of the room and stand before the large crowd. With the showcase mantle and fireplace as my dramatic backdrop, I will read the Latin phrase (careful to get those tricky vowels just right), offer a brief and poignant explanation, and then drop the mic. At least that's how I see it in my mind's eye.

According to ceremony protocol, I have the advantage of following K—'s slideshow. It's a carefully prepared synopsis of K—'s time at Whetstone, complete with Ken Burns styled transitions and music chosen just for the occasion. Even the other boys pay close attention for the ten minutes that it takes to show his journey from frowning and frumpy to smiling and serene.

It's nice. And no one tries to hide back the tears. But I like the slideshow for another reason. I like it because it is the perfect harbinger of this boy's life to come.

This is because almost without fail, the slideshow experiences some sort of "technical difficulty." Whether it's the antiquated computer, the unreliable rural internet, the beleaguered projector, or just the crunch of being pressed for time, the presentation never goes exactly as Axel plans.

But that's what makes it so moving, at least for me. It's an ironic foreshadowing of life to come. Nothing ever goes exactly like we plan, and this seems especially true when we have been planning for a long time. There's just more pressure. There is more that can go wrong and in more ways than we can imagine. This young man's life is not going to go like he thinks. And that's okay. Often, things work out even better that way.

Eventually, of course, the glitches get worked out and the slideshow glides to an end, the last picture a portrait of K—, still hanging on the projector screen, larger than life. It will be the one that we frame and put on the wall outside my office where all graduation photos are displayed.

The crowd is poised. It's my turn.

I step forward from the back, picking my way through the crowd of benches and dining room chairs assembled in front of me.

I pause, adjust my glasses, and look down at my card. I rub the top of my head for effect. Channeling my best Marcus Aurelius voice, I read: "*Cum grano salis.*"

It's Latin for "with a grain of salt."

The gist of this phrase, as I explain, is that we should maintain a healthy amount of skepticism and caution in order to find balance. To the ancient Romans, salt symbolized wisdom because it made the bitterness of life easier to swallow. "If you're wise," I hear myself saying to K—, "you'll learn to digest most things with a grain of salt. You, and your parents, will get through the difficult days ahead if you don't take each other too seriously. By all means, use the advice you have been given here at Whetstone, but take even that with a grain of salt, and season it for your circumstance. That's the difference between knowledge and wisdom. *Cum grano salis.*"

It's a bit of a stretch, and I haven't done enough research in my limited preparation time to know that it's not a pseudo-etymology, but I think it'll do.

I hand him the white index card and pull him in close for a hug.

Finally, as things draw to a close, people start shaking hands and making promises to stay in touch. Parents and staff snap last-minute photos on their phones. The last crumbs of cake are nibbled at, and hot coffee is poured for the road.

Outdoors, K— takes one last ceremonial disc golf shot, hoping to make a hole-in-one and pocket one hundred bucks. Indoors, he wipes his name from the chore board.

A box spilling with memories and a few bags of clothes are thrown into the back of a van, and *whoosh!* a young man heads back home, ready to tackle the *terra incognita*.

Chapter 3

April Fools

Axel

Once a year my wife, Christine, and I load up our four kids in whatever collision-only vehicle we happen to be driving at the time and travel somewhere within a very special geographical triangle. Its three corners are Pomona, Missouri; Chapel Hill, North Carolina; and Lexington, Kentucky. These are the hometowns of three couples who met at Harding University in Searcy, Arkansas, back when Kurt Cobain was still making great grunge records.

We call our rendezvous "SLP," which takes the first letter of each family's last name: Smith, Liimatta, and Paden. We look forward to this reunion all year long because it is a time to reconnect and to remember who we really are beneath the debt, degrees, and dirty diapers we have piled up in the years since graduating together. In simple company, we remind each other that life is about love and loyalty and laughter. We swap stories, share wisdom, and confess our faults. After two decades, there is very little we don't know about each other, and I think it is this transparency, more than anything else, that keeps us coming back. There is no pretending at SLP.

On Easter Weekend in 2015, we had gathered our little circus of fourteen at a rented condo in downtown St. Louis. The Zoo, the Arch, and Ted Drewes Frozen Custard were all on the to-do list. But at the very top was something called the City Museum.

For those who do not know, the City Museum is a hidden gem, or as I overheard one person around these parts say, "a heeden geem." Beyond this, I will defer to its website which bids you to venture within its 600,000 square feet and explore an "eclectic mixture of children's playground, funhouse, surrealistic pavilion, and architectural marvel made out of unique, found objects." The museum opened in 1997, "to the riotous approval of young and old alike!"

Very few things live up to their billings, much less those that are self-proclaimed. The City Museum, however, knows no hyperbole.

In ancient days, people would speak in hushed tones of the Seven Wonders of the World. The bucket list, before the bucket list was a thing. But if the people who visited the Hanging Gardens of Babylon on a weekend jaunt had been able to bring their seven-year-old to the City Museum, there would be one Wonder of the World and seven other Pretty Cool Things to See.

Soon after entering the museum, around 9:00 on the morning of Good Friday, I received a call from Jeremy Thompson, our executive director at Whetstone Boys Ranch. The signal was weak, so I split from the group and wandered into a quiet section dedicated to preserving the craftsmanship and artistic glory of late nineteenth century St. Louis. I strolled among architectural fragments from centuries past, trying to get a better connection.

I am tall and slim, with dark brown hair combed back and parted somewhere near the middle. I try to stand straight, but pictures usually show that I hunch a little, my shoulders pushed forward like I'm in a constant state of grading papers, which has felt like the case at times in twenty-four years of teaching. I said I strolled earlier, but that probably wasn't the case. I'm a pretty fast walker, impatient to a fault with the pace of people who stroll.

In this room full of relics, Jeremy informed me that an F2 tornado had struck Whetstone, and all five residents were in the process of being picked up by their parents. I would not even have time to drive back and say goodbye.

Bent over with the phone pressed to my ear, I wanted to make sure I understood what had happened and what was happening . . . without me. Would the boys need their schoolwork? What about transcripts? Had the school room been damaged? What about the library? Four years earlier, I had moved west to help start the ranch. On a tight non-profit budget, I had scraped together a collection of furniture, supplies, and teaching materials that connected with troubled boys. Was anything left?

I checked my phone for the date. April 3rd. Not April 1st, but perhaps just close enough to justify one last prank on an absent teacher's day off.

But no. This was no joke.

Jeremy went on to tell me that while there was serious damage to the first and second floors, the school in the large walkout basement was safe. Moisture would be an issue, but there wasn't much I could do about that. My school room, like the boys who had been hiding in the ping pong room next to it, had been saved. And since there was no need to rush home, I continued to drift among the reassembled ruins of the City Museum. Our college reunion would stay together, while the ranch was falling apart.

At first, each exhibit reminded me of tornado wreckage, a haunting montage of archeological rubble. Every corner revealed a new and disturbing image of dismemberment and someone else's broken dreams.

But as the day wore on, the pain lessened. Slowly, I sensed that the smiles all around me would not exist without the tearing down of one thing and the building up of something new and entirely unpredictable. With our young, small, and much more flexible children, we explored the Fungeon in the basement. On the first floor, we crawled through the Enchanted Caves. On the second, we got lost in the Hall of Mirrors, climbed through the twisting lumber jungle called Monstrocity, and navigated the collection of oddities contained within the Vault Room. For lunch we shared pizza in a café that mashes a rain forest with an art deco ballroom. On the third floor, we stitched together works of art from paper and plastic scraps in a make-shift studio called Art City. We wandered through the Museum of Mirth, Mystery and Mayhem, took a spin through Skateless Park and whizzed down Monster Slide. I was particularly struck by the jugglers in Everyday Circus. From what I could tell, they were artists in residence, trained to take daily stock of life's odd bits and find a place for them in their sweaty performance art. The strangeness of all the exhibits and the detachment I felt from the devastation at the ranch seemed the very essence of surreal.

Winding our way to the tenth floor, our three families met atop a giant slide repurposed from the riveted sheet metal delivery system connecting every level of the one-time shoe factory. An industrial machine and assembly line that had produced bootstraps for soldiers in World War II was now being used by parents and their children to produce screams of sheer delight.

And finally, on the flat roof where there resides a transplanted planetarium dome, a Ferris wheel, and a school bus whose front wheels dangle off the dizzying edge, I gazed out upon the face of the great French city and took a deep breath.

The air was cool and sweet compared to the stuffy and odor-filled museum. Here, I could look out. Here, at the top of a long, hard climb, I turned my eyes to the horizon where the amber-rose sky silhouetted clean, steel lines. Thousands of smooth, glass windows reflected the warm light of the setting sun.

Here, under the watchful eye of a twenty-four-foot praying mantis that crowns a museum full of broken things, my thoughts turned towards the ranch and of all that needed rescuing there.

Unaware

Cows bundle
and back into fences.

Birds tuck into hedges,
bunched on the lee.

Hissing barn cats
not on speaking terms
squeeze into the same
tiny space.

The signs are all around
for those with eyes to see.

How strange then,
to be on the blindside,
still, and without clue—

while nature
prepares
without awareness.

CALL

"Follow Me..."

Follow me, and let the dead bury their own dead.

MATTHEW 8:22

Chapter 4

Flowmaster

Michelle

I've always loved a guy in a truck.

So it came as no surprise to me when I met my future husband, Ty, in the parking lot of a Taco Bell in Riverhead, New York. His Dodge RAM rumbled, featuring a Flowmaster performance exhaust system.

The rendezvous at Taco Bell was necessary for two girls navigating the streets of New York for the first time. And it marked the first date for Ty and me—a blind one, arranged by his sister who had driven with me in my much smaller and quieter S-10, all the way from Rochester, Michigan.

At the time Ty worked as a house parent at Timothy Hill Children's Ranch, a transitional living home, on Long Island. I knew this because he was receiving the 2004 Volunteer of the Year Award that evening. I hoped I had kept my dress wrinkle-free during the five-hundred-mile drive.

After dropping off my vehicle at Timothy Hill, we changed into our formal wear, and the three of us squeezed into the front seat of Ty's truck. His sister acted as a buffer between two strangers on their first date.

It's a really funny picture, as I look back on it. Ty and I barely spoke two words the entire drive. What do you say to a cute guy, driving a cool truck, who also happens to be Volunteer of the Year?

We arrived at the venue a few minutes late because of traffic, the kind I had only seen in movies. The three of us strode to the head table in front of three hundred people. Most of these nicely dressed individuals, I understood, were pretty serious donors to Timothy Hill. The point of the dinner was to show gratitude and appreciation for them.

As if being on a blind date, three states from home, wasn't enough pressure.

If you're getting the sense that the cards were stacked against us, you're right. I felt the same way.

And then a funny thing happened. A magical thing.

Ty and I started talking. And laughing. At the head table, with all those important leaders and guest speakers and honored guests, we started swapping stories about growing up. Mine centered on Indiana, soccer, showing sheep, and falling off horses. His revolved around Texas, golf, turf, manure, and *riding* horses.

At one point, I threw out a line about wanting to be a stay-at-home mom because I did . . . but also because I could tell he valued that sort of thing. I remember wanting him to see me as nurturing and maternal.

I was already thinking marriage.

We were not an official couple, just an hour into our first date, when Jerry Hill, founder of Timothy Hill Children's Ranch, put his arms around Ty and me and said, "You two sure do make a nice couple."

Ty and I locked eyes, laughed and said thank you, each hoping his words might prove prophetic.

A lot has changed since that first date on Long Island, fifteen years ago. Ty's sister no longer sits between us. We finished college. We got married. We added four kids. We moved out to Arizona to manage a golf course. We journeyed to Mountain View, Missouri, to serve as house parents for Whetstone.

We might not laugh as much as we did on that first date because that's not the way life works. But one thing has stayed the same.

We always ride together.

Chapter 5

Corn Dogs

Matt

My Whetstone journey began during a volunteer week at Timothy Hill Children's Ranch in 2002. The same ranch where Ty and Michelle first met. It was there that I first met two guys who wanted to start a ranch someday, something called Whetstone Boys Ranch. It was nothing but a dream then. I know this because they had hats that proclaimed "Whetstone, Not Just a Dream." Actual hats.

I now wear one of those hats. In fact, I wear several. We often joke around here that I am the "programathist." I am equal parts program director and therapist, which causes its share of conflicting interests. I often find myself disagreeing with myself . . . vehemently.

If I think about it for a few seconds, I can probably name a dozen different official positions I have held in the last decade, along with another dozen unofficial ones. All of them required a lot of on-the-job training to overcome my beginner's ignorance. You don't know what you don't know.

Nowhere is this more true than in the counseling profession. Ulysses Everett McGill is correct in *O Brother Where Art Thou*, when he says that "It's a fool that looks for logic in the chambers of the human heart."

Still, I have found that if we stumble around together for

long enough, answers and patterns emerge. God shows up.

One of my fondest memories from my time at Timothy Hill involved telling a group of boys that I planned to eat some fresh eggs the chickens had just laid.

A chorus of criticism erupted. "You can't eat that. It just came out of that chicken's butt!" they yelled.

"Where do you think eggs come from?" I asked.

Stone-faced and matter-of-factly, one boy said, "They make them in the back of the store. That's why they're white and clean and not that nasty brown."

They'd never seen chickens before. Or horses. Most had never seen dogs other than pit bulls or Rottweilers. So I guess it stands to reason they might think that a chicken poops out an egg.

On another occasion, I carried on a long conversation with a resident about the relative merits of corn dogs, or "Cajun popsicles" as my uncle fondly called them. This kid loved corn dogs more that anyone I'd ever met, and all his mom could afford was cheap frozen food from the food desert surrounding her home. Those corn dogs were a staple for his family.

Now there's nothing inherently wrong with a good corn dog. I'm on record boasting my affection for them. They're dinner and dessert in one package. And if you've never tasted anything better, there shouldn't be any shame in loving them like this boy did. Still, I decided he deserved to taste a real steak dinner from real steak house—nothing fancy, just a properly prepared sirloin with a baked potato…and some silverware. It was a meal that many of us would take for granted.

He went on and on about that $12 steak, like it had been prepared at a five-star restaurant. It's not his fault that corn dogs were his only point of comparison.

One of the greatest honors of that job at Timothy Hill was taking a group of young men to buy new suits. For many of them, it was their first. Typically, we rose early on MLK day and dressed up in our slick new threads. We went out for breakfast, listened to an inspirational speaker, and then came back for our annual game of cut-throat Monopoly, still dressed to the nines.

It was a professional, knock-down-drag-out tournament and an apt demonstration of how the "apparel oft proclaims the man."

They behaved like men because we treated them like men.

Eventually, I left the children's ranch and went back to school to study marriage and family therapy at Harding University in Searcy, Arkansas. I worked at Capstone Treatment Center, also in Searcy, where I trained extensively in trauma, addiction, attachment, and canine therapy.

But I'm not sure that any of this prepared me for a career in counseling any better than living alongside young men who, much like myself, were learning how to do something or think something or be something for the very first time.

Chapter 6

SPACE HELMETS

Axel

I was born on June 1st, 1974, in Pontiac, Michigan. First child of Anne and Fred Liimatta, first grandchild on my mother's Dahlstrom side, and about middle of the pack on the *paterfamilias*—although my grandfather, having died in a tragic construction accident when a giant dirt scoop pinned him to the ground, was not around to meet me. And I never knew Grandma Liimatta either since she died in a car accident within a year of my birth. Point being, I had the love and attention a firstborn divines as his birthright, along with a sense that it could all be taken away from me in the blink of an eye.

My dad has always been real keen on real talk about death. In addition to losing both of his parents while young, he served his country as a Green Beret during Vietnam, working as a Special Forces medic during the war's deadliest period and earning decorations he still won't really talk about. Upon returning home (without his country's welcome) he worked in an ambulance as a first responder, putting his unique set of skills to work in civilian service. None of this did much for his sense of security before he started having children of his own. I guess he felt the need to prepare us for the inevitable.

Despite all of this, my dad can be a real ham. When I was growing up, my father once wore a plastic space helmet for the church directory photo, prompting one naive observer to comment on how sweet it was for my family to let our "special needs uncle" sit with us for the family photo.

On the inside, however, my father has often struggled with depression and anger. Rage really. Intense emotions that move like lava through his veins and, which when I was young, would occasionally erupt and cover us all in fiery ash.

My military career is encapsulated by a grueling two months as a cadet at The United States Military Academy at West Point. Space cadet I should say . . . or rather not say since that would be engaging in the sort of negative self-talk we try to avoid around Whetstone.

Do as I say, not as I do.

I am a very skilled self-beater-upper. It's like the highway of my inner monologue is filled with overpass signs that say, "You just missed your exit!" I have to speed my way to the next one—always a longer distance than that between normal exits. The entire time I'm moving faster and angrier in the wrong direction, and I'm hammering the top of the steering wheel and yelling, "You're such an idiot!"

At West Point, I was what those in the military call a "spaz." If you've seen *A Few Good Men,* Aaron Sorkin's courtroom drama about military hazing, I was Marine Private William Santiago. I didn't fit in. I didn't talk right, walk right, eat right, or dress right. And while every new cadet feels like this during basic training (aptly named Beast Barracks), I was an extreme case.

I had no military background. To that point in my life, I had never shot a gun or shined a shoe. I wouldn't say I was sheltered exactly—I spent eighteen years surrounded by the urban decay of Pontiac, Michigan—but my set of experiences did not exactly align with those of my classmates.

From the first bus ride to campus—when I tried to introduce myself (I think I may have missed the "no talking" sign plastered on the stone faces all around me)—to my departure two months later, I was subjected to an unending barrage of insults.

This was something I was not used to. I had grown

accustomed to people thinking I was pretty swell. At West Point, this assumption about myself was called into serious question and in the most adamant of terms.

I knew this was part of breaking me down so the military could build me back up again, but one month into the process, I was pretty certain the demolition phase would not end until there was nothing left of me.

I remember standing on our hands in the shower and being told we'd have the cleanest butt holes in the company. Not exactly something to write home about.

I remember cutting a pie into nine slightly uneven pieces and then becoming the center of attention in a mess hall that seats over one thousand cadets. It felt like upper classmen from a football field away were leaping tables to get a glimpse of my pathetic handiwork. Not a very dignified scene in the grandiose hall still echoing with the famous words from General McArthur's famous "Duty, Honor, Country" speech.

I remember being grilled in the quad about the designation of an O-6—just one of the hundreds of things new cadets are required to memorize from their Plebe Bibles, along with the definition of leather (*if the fresh skin of an animal, cleaned and divested of all hair, fat, and other extraneous matter, be immersed in a dilute solution of tannic acid, a chemical combination ensues . . .*) and the number of days until Army "beats" Navy.

"Staff sergeant, sir," I answered, over and over again. I just knew I was right.

"New cadet! What's an O-6?"

"Staff sergeant, sir." He called his friends over to ask me the same question. "Staff sergeant," I repeated to their unending glee. More upperclassman gathered.

Finally, someone had pity on me, quietly dropping the hint that I was repeating E-6. Fighting back tears, I corrected my mistake, "O-6 is colonel, sir." The crowd dispersed, leaving me alone with my shame.

Maybe it was the irony of my mistaking a staff sergeant for a colonel that got them all riled up. But I suspect it was just the spectacle of me being such a spaz.

Of course, I contributed mightily to the breaking-down process. I berated myself at every possible opportunity. I convinced myself I probably deserved the harsh treatment. All of which hastened my downward spiral. The spaz label colored the way I perceived myself (still does sometimes)—my every thought tinged with existential dread which to that point in my life I had only encountered in a high school reading of Kafka.

The worst part of my military tenure was an immobilizing catch-22. Stay and be reminded that I'm a screwup for not having the courage to leave? Or leave and be reminded that I'm a screwup for not having the courage to stay.

I know the boys at Whetstone feel the same way at times. Success can be failure; and failure can often be success.

My parents weren't much help. I got one ten-minute call each week, and they spent most of their energy trying to convince me that things weren't as bad as they seemed. I appreciated their effort, but I can't say it provided any comfort. What I really wanted was for someone to tell me I wasn't crazy, and that things really *were* that bad.

I had no advisors. No confidantes. The Bible, while vastly comforting in my darkest moments, seemed to offer conflicting advice on the topic. "I can do all things through Christ who strengthens me" on one hand. "Do nothing out of selfish ambition and vain conceit" on the other.

At the end of Beast Barracks, I recall staring at myself in the mirror for a good five minutes. Try it some time. You'll see some surprising things. What shocked me in that moment, scared me really, was that I didn't recognize myself.

I was becoming someone else. Someone I didn't like. This person had no sense of humor. He did not smile. He could not remember the last time he laughed. He could not remember how to laugh or any reasons to laugh.

And this, of all things, the man in the mirror found funny.

I saw my dad, in his space helmet. I saw his crazy, bug-eyed smile in that church directory. I heard his loud, room-ringing laughter.

I was built for joy.

And so I chose to leave. I left the free college education, the wild ambitions of my youth, and the accolades I had received from a proud community which reveled in my nomination and appointment to the nation's most prestigious military academy.

I could no longer justify my misery by balancing it with other people's happiness.

But even then, I knew I did not leave West Point to go on a selfish quest for personal fulfillment or to do what made me feel "happy." Deep down I desired a vocation, what Frederick Buechner defines as a calling where "your greatest joy meets the world's greatest need."

I think this is why I became a teacher and why I came to Whetstone.

Some days this means introducing a boy to Fleetwood Mac for the first time.

On others, it means listening to him read a poem that he is proud to have written and shared with others.

On really good days, it means debating the merits and demerits of a film or a book and realizing that he is starting to form his own original thoughts about truth and beauty, about right and wrong.

And on those days when it feels like things are spinning out of control, and my school room feels like the inside of an asteroid-ridden space shuttle, I just put on my cheap plastic helmet . . . and smile my toothiest smile.

CHAOS

"Lord, Save Us!"

Lord, save us! We're going to drown!
MATTHEW 8:25

Chapter 7

ALERT

Axel

The evening of April 2, 2015 was like most at Whetstone. School, which is administered on campus in a retrofitted basement, ended at 3:30. The five boys living here at the time marched up two flights of stairs to their rooms and changed into their running clothes. They gathered with staff on the front porch for a quick stretch before running two miles along the winding, dirt road leading to and from the ranch.

Upon their return, the boys logged their time, downed some water and a piece of fruit, then moved right into a game of pick-up basketball on the small concrete court next to our large garage/woodshop.

Minor disagreements whirled up among the young men, common after and during such exercise—tiny dust devils that kick up from time to time. But nothing came of it, and the boys showered, changed into comfort clothing, and began preparations for dinner.

Memory of this meal has passed into oblivion by all accounts, but one can be relatively sure the crock pot had been hard at work because Joey and Troy, two twenty-somethings, were in charge that evening.

Joey is small but strong. Think of a scaled-down version of John Cena, the WWE wrestler. Tattoos run up and down both of Joey's forearms. You'd hate to go toe-to-toe in a steel cage with him. He sports a thick beard, maybe in subconscious protest to U.S. Marine protocol since he is no longer bound by its dress code. Marines are like that—fiercely proud and protective of the Corps but instinctively indignant towards its rules. Just ask a former Marine if he kept any of the military-issue "items" after serving his term. You're likely to get dancing eyes and a mischievous smile in return.

Troy is the opposite. Tall and clean-shaven, save the usual scruff that an unmarried man wears as his badge of honor. Troy played basketball at Harding University for a year before dropping out and then working construction on Long Island. He knew Matt at Timothy Hill and was recruited by him to serve as mentoring specialist before Joey, whom Troy had recruited to replace himself. Troy had been retained as evening staff after his year in that position.

They had been buddies back in Long Island, New York, and both had been called to Whetstone to work with struggling teenagers because their story was not too different. They had been in our boys' shoes not too long ago.

Both Joey and Troy remember that April evening as being unremarkable, par for the troubled teen course—which is to say there were a few relational landmines to navigate, some minor explosions with limited collateral damage, and one or two applications of emotional first aid. But there were no official casualties.

Joey recalls that everyone was a bit on edge, and during the evening group time called "highs and lows," he encouraged the boys to just "make it till Friday evening" when they would visit Pizza Americana in Willow Springs (a local joint that has served us free pizza once a week since we opened), play a few games of pool, and then return for a good movie in our theatre/basement/school room.

Joey and Troy shuttled the boys to bed a bit early that night, around 8:30. They administered evening medications and guided the boys through teeth-brushing and other nighttime rituals.

Close to 9:30, lights went out. Whispered conversations continued for another fifteen minutes or so until Troy and Joey passed the baton to Thomas, the night staff at the time, whose job was to maintain calm and quiet. Not too hard for a 6'5" bear of a man who sits awake in the hall for eight hours and checks each room every fifteen minutes.

All was quiet.

Now that Thomas was in charge, Joey returned to his quarters. A decorated combat veteran of Operation *Iraqi Freedom*, he was keenly aware of an approaching storm, having received weather updates on his phone throughout the evening. He double and triple-checked his survival gear as well as the backpacks the boys had assembled during their survival skills training course—the next installment of which was planned for the coming Saturday. He felt prepared for every eventuality, including but not limited to EMP and zombie apocalypse.

Though he knew Thomas was awake, Joey kept a watchful eye for a couple hours before nodding off to sleep.

The weather radio was in place. His phone was set to *Alert*.

Chapter 8

Chainsaws

Joey Padovano (mentoring specialist)

12:39 a.m. I am rudely awakened by an alert system from the weather radio in my room. The low-pitched but loud vibration is closely followed by the same alert from my cell phone, their alternating sounds spurring me into action.

Automatically, I fall into the routine of putting on my clothes and grabbing my gear, a methodical action I learned as a Marine on a MEDEVAC team. The familiarity of the scenario makes me smirk as I roll out of bed.

A tornado warning has been issued for the following counties:
Texas . . .
Boots, check . . .
Oregon . . .
Flashlight, check . . .
Shannon . . .
Lucky knife, check . . .
Howell . . .
Lucky—"Whoa! That's us!"

I pick up the radio and head for the door. Thomas, the night staff, is just outside my door on his computer, and I ask him to check the radar. Nothing but a big cloud of red surrounding a blue GPS dot.

Okay, this could be for real.

I wake up all the boys and tell them to grab shoes and blankets. Seconds later, five heads poke out of their doorways. They are waiting to hear what's going on from the guy dressed like he is about to go backpacking in the dark.

As the words come out of my mouth, I realize my voice shakes. I take a deep breath and proceed slowly.

"There is some nasty weather headed our way, and we're gonna ride this out in the basement."

Not a peep.

Thomas and I hand out survival packs to each boy, acquired during the wilderness course I teach. These packs are filled with different tools, each representing a unique skill: paracord, a make-shift tourniquet, and a flashlight, along with a half-dozen other things if a guy has been here long enough.

Once we load the boys down with their gear, Thomas leads the way and I follow behind. The boys are very quiet. I do a head count and make one last glance into my room to see if there is something I forgot.

Oh, yeah. My dog! He comes right when I call, but suddenly, at the bottom of the stairs he pees.

I can see that his leg quivers just as the power goes out.

With my flashlight guiding us, we navigate four flights of stairs, multiple doors and corners, until we reach the ping pong room in the basement. A leg injury hampers one boy, and he hobbles down the steps much slower than everyone would like.

In the ping pong room, there are no windows, and we are several walls removed from the outside. There are also no beds. The boys each find a corner and settle down. A few wrangle some chairs from the adjoining hallway and schoolroom.

"What did the weather radio say?" T— asks. He is an older boy from a Midwest state, but he seems more anxious than the rest. Perhaps it's because he's more aware of what could happen. The younger ones are oblivious. For all they know, this is an adventure and I am Gandalf.

T— is thinking about Gollum.

Once everyone seems settled, I leave Thomas in charge and make one more trip upstairs to open the front door and look out, listening for nearby thunder.

It is eerily quiet.

I wonder if I should move my truck from where it is parked beneath a large walnut tree and put it in front of the garage in case the tree falls over. In the silence, I decide against it and return to the basement, where I find boys cracking jokes and trying to find ways to use the current situation to get out of doing morning chores and schoolwork.

"I don't think Axel will allow a tornado to cancel school," M— suggests.

They have taken to calling Mr. Liimatta by his first name when he isn't around, a hard habit to break since his name is rather fun to say.

"Yeah, no way, cuz the tornado would probably forget to say 'please' or 'sir'."

They all laugh. M— stands up and starts walking around the room like Mr. Liimatta, doing his best to keep himself straight and calling himself, "Sir Axel." He drapes one of the green sleeping bags we have pulled from a storage closet around his shoulders and starts swinging an imaginary sword.

"Be gone, ye comma splice!" he shouts.

With my cell phone I call everyone I know in the area, a very short list at the time, and tell them we are in the basement. They should get somewhere safe, too. I make a point to call the program director Matt, who lives offsite, and we agree to check in once the storm system passes, just to make sure everyone is okay.

Having been on the move for thirty minutes, I sit down and take a quick breath. I am prepared to wait a while. My phone tells me it's 1:09 a.m.

Moments later, the whole house begins to shake, and every boy instinctively curls into his corner of the room. One jumps under the ping pong table. They use the sleeping bags to cover their heads.

It is shocking to see how quickly the mood goes from joking and laughing, to panic and fear.

Directly above our heads, it sounds like the Incredible Hulk is stomping through the house and hurling anything he can get his hands on.

Will the walls collapse? Will the ceiling crumble?

The boys are curled up tight.

The Hulk continues his rampage for 10 seconds? 30 seconds? A minute?

Later on, we cannot agree on a time.

Afterwards, the boys, Thomas, and I look at each other but say nothing. What can be said? Our hearts are in our throats and in our eyes.

I wait for my breath to return then cautiously tiptoe up the stairs, clueless about what might greet me. I hope a green monster is not waiting to pounce.

The door to the ground floor is blocked. I put my shoulder into it. And again. The door inches open, and I keep shoving, eventually coming to the realization that I'm pushing a piano that has moved fifteen feet.

I squeeze myself through into the upstairs.

At this moment, time freezes.

I stare in awe, unsuccessfully trying to process what I am seeing. The piercing sound of the house alarm is going off, a steady stream of water pours down from the second story into the living room, and the evening breeze blows through the entire house.

But I am still not processing what has happened.

Flashes of lightening suddenly reveal the rubble and debris that surrounds me. This is not Whetstone. If so, it has been transformed into a battle zone. More flashes reveal the front lines of a fire fight. I am back in BDU's and combat boots, bracing for what is yet to come with my rifle in hand. For a few interminable seconds, I am back in Iraq.

Mechanically, I walk up the stairs to the second floor, the high intensity beam of my LED flashlight leading the way. At the top, I stare down the hallway that leads to the boys' rooms. My eyes flood with tears of terror and relief.

The hallway is completely blocked by furniture from our rooms. Heavy bed frames built by a volunteer group from

Kentucky. Oak dressers and drawers. Cabinets, wardrobes, and chairs. Mattresses have been sucked out of the windows, and the walls are blasted with what looks like shrapnel.

I have seen buildings leveled from airstrikes, but this is different. It is worse. There is no doubt in my mind that all of us would have been seriously injured, and some most likely killed if we hadn't holed up in the basement.

I snap back to reality when I hear a loud hissing. I point my spotlight out of a gaping hole in the side of the house to discover the source is a 500-gallon propane tank that remains, miraculously, behind the concrete base of a six-car garage that no longer exists.

It sticks out like a hitchhiker's thumb.

Beyond the tank, I see what remains of a two-story hay barn, which has been leveled as well.

Every vehicle in the parking lot is smashed, including my truck that I *almost* moved. I assess the sky, smell the breeze, and then, the faint but undeniable odor of propane. This is not over. It starts to dawn on me that we will not leave here for safety on our own.

1:21 a.m. My first call is to the fire department to inform them of the situation. This is followed by a call to Matt and then several phone calls to friends I talked to earlier. With each ring of the phone, I become increasingly worried that the person on the other end won't pick up. Some families have nowhere to hide but a closet on the first floor. This is the first time I think there might be people who aren't as lucky as we are.

When I make my last phone call, the faint sound of chainsaws is buzzing in the distance. First responders and neighbors are already engaged in the back-breaking work of making their way through the debris to get to us.

Help is on the way, but gas may be filling the house, and I still don't know if it is safe to leave. On the other hand, we have no choice *but* to leave.

The risk of staying where we are has now surpassed the risk of moving.

When I finally return to the boys in the basement, their eyes are fixed on me and their ears are waiting to hear what I will say. This is a drastic change from the usual attempts required to lasso their attention.

"We're safe for the moment," I hear myself saying, "but we can't stay here anymore."

Then, in a single file line we all march out of the house together, survival packs secured around our shoulders.

In the military, the word "recover" means to get back up. Like after a session of doing pushups until you reach muscle failure and collapse; or after being pinned down from a firefight and then getting up to push forward. It is a word always used with intensity. *Recover!* This is so that everyone knows what is at stake. We must recover, I tell myself.

With all of the boys now outside, I take the position as point man. Thomas covers the rear. A soft whimper escapes M—, the boy who had just been dancing around, pretending to be Mr. Liimatta. I can feel the boys looking around, processing the magnitude of what we have just survived. Several boys gasp. Then a few "Oh My Gods." I don't think this qualifies as taking the Lord's name in vain. I am thinking the same thing myself. "My God, My God . . ."

I do what I can to distract the young men from the damage, afraid that they will freak out if they realize how close we really came to death. But it is impossible to avoid. We climb through seventy-foot trees lying on the ground. Later on, one of the boys describes the downed power lines we walked around as "slithering black snakes ready to strike at any given moment."

Do I really think the boys won't notice?

Looking behind me, I can count everyone by the number of bouncing headlamp beams. Thankfully, there are six. We tramp toward our destination, the large red metal pole barn still standing about one hundred yards away.

As we close in on the barn, the chainsaws grow louder.

Chapter 9

Covers

Michelle

My husband, Ty, and I woke up to hail pounding the roof of our home in Peace Valley. Our three young boys slept in the room next to us and didn't stir.

The small unincorporated town of Peace Valley, population 447, sits on a narrow two-lane blacktop, Highway W, about fifteen miles from Whetstone Ranch.

Ty and I had just purchased the home. In fact, this was only our second night in the "getaway" house, as we called it. The nickname exemplified our need to protect our family from the stress that accompanied being house parents at a therapeutic boys ranch.

We had decided on an underground house, safe from tornados—the ones that rip up trees from their roots and the ones, like boys, that rip through everything in their teenage sights. You need your own grounding when you're a houseparent, a safe place, or you'll get sucked into the vortex. Our new Peace Valley home was our shelter from a variety of storms. Our home away from home.

At 1:23 a.m., I received the text.

A tornado had delivered a direct hit to the Ranch.

And in that moment, despite all of our attempts to be grounded, our first thought was that we needed to be there. We felt bad that we weren't, and even though this doesn't really make any sense, the twister felt like our fault. Maybe if we had been there . . .

We needed to see our ranch boys.

With thunder still rumbling in the distance, we decided that Ty would go to the ranch alone. He didn't have his phone, so he took mine, handed me a loaded handgun that I had never shot before, and headed for Whetstone. Hypothetically, I would use this weapon to protect myself from anyone who would mess with me in the middle of the country and without a car. Looters maybe? I don't really know what we were thinking.

But then again, the first neighbor we met, less than a week before the tornado, had greeted us at her door with a shotgun.

As Ty drove off, I lay in bed alone, wide awake, the pistol under his pillow. Moments later, I heard the mushy sound of gravel. With muddy boots and a half-grin, my husband met me in the kitchen. We then loaded three pajama-clothed kids into our Suburban and drove off to face whatever lay in store, together.

About one mile from the ranch, and with our windows rolled *up*, we were struck by the unmistakable smell of cedar. It was overwhelming, really—resulting from hundreds of snapped trees whose strong scent swept towards us and grew stronger each moment.

Soon we were at a standstill, our voyage blocked by dense debris which firemen, their red and yellow reflecting in our headlights, worked to clear. Ty instinctively jumped out and offered his help.

Within minutes, however, he walked back to the Suburban, carrying something across his chest. Upon reaching us, he turned it around so that I could recognize the Whetstone sign that formerly hung at the entrance to the ranch. It was badly mangled and had landed here, a quarter mile from the ranch. That's when it really hit me. This really happened.

After each clearing, the fire truck pulled forward and allowed us to drive a few feet closer. After an hour and a half, we had finally crawled all the way to the house, too late to see the boys.

Thankfully, Joey had not left. Along with our three boys, Ty and I exited our Suburban and picked our way through the maze of downed walnut trees to greet the mentoring specialist hero on the porch, with huge hugs.

He had done it. He made the right call that night. He kept the boys safe. He was safe. I squeezed him tighter as these thoughts rushed through me.

With more storms likely, trucks of all shapes and sizes began to arrive.

As they did so, the scene became increasingly bizarre. Joey told us his version of the night's drama and that the boys, loaded down with blankets, had been piled into a church van and driven through the carnage to Pomona Church, where they would stay the night.

Beyond that we knew nothing.

Chapter 10

SMALL

Matt

I was safe, standing in nothing but my underwear, staring in amazement out of a window at my home. Lightning crashed, thunder boomed. Wind pressed against the side of the small house my wife and I rented. The structure creaked and moaned under the weight. Still, I remained glued to the sliding glass door—caught up in the tempest.

Not in the way you rubberneck at a wreck, curious as to what might have happened. Not in the way some get caught up in movie explosions, in bleeding headlines, enthused and inspired to go out and match the rage. Not even in the way we sometimes appreciate the splendor of majestic things . . .

It was a small feeling. Actually, it was the enormous feeling of being small and insignificant, but content. I could've watched the storm for the rest of the night, sheltered in my little house.

Then came the call.

The voice on the other end of the line was steady and shaky, rattled and composed. The call came from the ranch. There was no denying a direct hit.

Two hours later, I was trapped, just around the bend, maybe

a quarter mile from the ranch. Beside me sat Brandon Maxwell, the ranch's site director, who had hitched a ride. A co-founder of the ranch in 2011, he was eager and nervous to see what damage had been done.

The ride in did not give us much hope.

Still, a balmy freshness pervaded the night. If you could get past the erratic flashlights, screaming chainsaws, incessant beeping of machines, and the impassioned cries of rescue workers, the spectacle was quite gorgeous. The pace of our crawl afforded me this luxury of observation.

My reverie was interrupted by the fire chief's truck, which ground to a halt on my passenger side, a once-lofty wire now wrapped around its axle, its emergency lights continuing to turn in crazy circles.

How many live wires had *we* driven over?

We could do nothing but wait for the road to clear. We were dependent on a caring group of strangers with the proper tools and a unique set of skills who were able to clear the road back. We couldn't do it ourselves no matter how hard we might have tried.

It's a humbling thing to wait on someone else to do the job you think you're supposed to be able to do.

If you've ever experienced that feeling, then you have a small sense of what it's like to pull up to Whetstone Boys Ranch, far down a dirt road in the middle of what seems like nowhere, to drop off your son with a caring crew of complete strangers—to know that even though your child sits three feet behind you in the back seat of your own car, he's miles away with a forest of immovable wreckage blocking the road.

Chapter 11

Donuts

M— (a resident during the night of the tornado)

Arriving at Pomona Christian Church on the morning after the tornado, all five of us boys were treated to a surprise—donuts! Powdered, glazed, sprinkled, the works. I think I tried a little bit of everything because it's hard not to eat your emotions after a near-death experience.

Come to think of it, is there anything more comforting than a donut in times of trouble?

After all of us had a little more than our fair share, we started to feel restless and anxious. Not surprising if you consider our sugar intake, but I think the barrage of questions would have come regardless.

"Is the ranch shut down?"
"Was anyone hurt or killed?"
"Are the cows okay? The pigs? The cats? The dogs?"
"Do my parents know what happened?"
"What's the plan for today?"
"Is school cancelled?"
"Can I have another donut?"

The answer to each of these questions, predictably, was more food! And since we were close to West Plains this meant the Ozark Cafe. It's the kind of place a farmer or railroad worker grabs a coffee and an egg sandwich before the rest of the world hits its first snooze.

Breakfast included all the usual suspects: eggs, bacon, sausage, pancakes, hash browns, grits, biscuits and gravy. You name it, we ate it. There was joking and nervous laughter as we began to process the previous night's events. It still felt very much like a dream . . .

The trip downstairs, the ping pong room, the monster upstairs, the dark hike to the barn, and the van ride to the church gymnasium where we stayed the night. Did all that really happen? Was I mixing it up with a TV show or movie I had watched recently? Not likely, since we don't get much of that at Whetstone.

After breakfast number two (*yes, teenagers count donuts as breakfast*) we made our way to the fire station for some Red Cross supplies: blankets, bottled water, a promise that they would visit the ranch soon and deliver more of the same, along with a new generator at no cost. It felt strange to be the recipient of such assistance after seeing so many other disaster victims served by the Red Cross workers on the news.

Disaster victim. I am a disaster victim? That sounds so weird. But I guess I am.

After loading everything into the van, we returned to Pomona Christian Church. Less than a mile from our destination, we were stopped by a train. We sat in silence as it rumbled by, its roar reminding us all of the thirty seconds we had spent in mortal danger, afraid for our lives, just a few hours ago. The locomotive passed on by, and we continued on without a single word spoken.

In the church parking lot, Mr. Foster told us that a local campground, Rock Garden, had offered to host us for the day. Our parents would pick us up before nightfall, and we were instructed to relax and try to have fun. There would be basketball, disc golf, volleyball, and, if we needed it, some peace and quiet.

I remember two things about that time, as we waited for our parents to arrive. The first was how much food kept streaming in as people heard about our predicament and rushed to bring us sustenance. It was as if everyone's first thought was, "Those boys are going to need something to eat." They were obviously unaware of the fact that we had already feasted like kings that morning and probably wouldn't need another meal until dinner.

But I get it. Food equals love. When we don't know what to say, we cook. When we don't know what to feel, we eat. It somehow seems like an answer to something.

The second memory is that of a beautiful acoustic guitar, a Gibson with wood inlays, given to me by Mr. Padovano. He visited us at Rock Garden to say his goodbyes, not knowing if or when he would see us again.

"I want you to have this, M—," he said. "Use it to keep your hands busy."

My parents picked me up from Rock Garden Christian Camp at about four in the afternoon. I was the last to leave, so I had the unique opportunity to observe the mixture of relief that everyone was safe, shock that Whetstone was shut down, and nervousness about what came next. On the whole, a near-death experience seemed to give everyone a renewed sense of appreciation for family, regardless of the strain.

As my ranchmates reunited with their families, my mind raced with questions about my own uncertain future.

"Would I ever see these guys again?"

"What would my parents say? What would I say?"

"Would I be sent to another ranch, or wilderness program, or treatment center?"

"What about school? What about my grades at Whetstone? What about the test I was planning to take this morning?"

The reunion with mom and dad was a bit anticlimactic. We hugged. They said they loved me. I did the same. It was pretty much what you might expect.

We loaded my new guitar into their car, which had just made the five-hundred-mile trip to Missouri, and then we drove to a local hotel.

Waking late, the next day we proceeded to the ranch to witness the damage for ourselves and to dig out anything of mine that might still be around.

The devastation started about seven miles from the ranch, faithfully following the road that leads right to the main building's doorstep. It seemed to me that the twister aimed for us. The car was eerily silent as my parents and I rolled up and down the hills on UU Highway, trying to process the tangles of barbed wire, fallen trees, shattered trailer homes, demolished roofs, and smashed vehicles.

When we finally rolled up to the ranch, I was dumbstruck.

Giant walnut trees were uprooted and carelessly thrown to the ground like someone had dropped a box of toothpicks. Once inside I was even more shocked at the missing furniture that had been sucked out of windows. Upstairs, splinters of glass were embedded into the walls of my bedroom. Not only windows but entire window frames were gone. It was sobering to think that I had been asleep in this room just a few hours ago.

I could not escape the feeling that someone was trying to tell me something.

CONTROL

"Why Are You So Afraid?"

You of little faith, why are you so afraid?
MATTHEW 8:26

Natura Magistra

Can nature
teach us grace?

Does storm
transform
the terror
in its face
when beauty
sits along
its path—
much less
such objects
fit for wrath?

Can earthquake,
hurricane,
or fire
relent,
reroute,
retract
their ire?

Or death,
most natural of all,
have mercy
on the small?

No, death,
it takes them first,
cuts down the pure
and spares the worst.

There is no love
in nature,
just power
pushing us to find
forgiveness
elsewhere.

Chapter 12

FALLEN

Axel

I had come with my family, after Sunday church, to get my first look at the post-tornado ranch. I hoped to address some of my survivor's guilt and to get eyes on what work would be like on Monday morning.

My three children, dressed in a collage of traditional Easter colors, explored the carnage like it was a jungle gym.

I took a few photographs of my kids at the end of the driveway, the devastation looking more like something produced with Photoshop than the unedited reality of photojournalism. Looking back, it seems strange that I would do this, but I couldn't help myself. It's been my job since the ranch opened in 2011 to document Whetstone's journey. And the irony of my kids in their vibrant Easter clothes was too alluring. The pictures, with their stark contrast of color and emotion (the children are of course smiling) are oddly surreal.

My enthusiastic seven-year-old boy standing in a giant hole left by an uprooted stump.

My two sweet-faced girls poking out of a cedar post frame where the Whetstone sign had hung three days earlier.

All three of them standing together on the concrete slab that previously served as the foundation for a garage that housed hundreds of tools, agricultural implements, and pieces of recreational equipment. It was once a safe place for everything we had collected in three and half years of operation. Some of it I assumed helpers had reclaimed and stored in the metal pole barn that survived. But many of these items—most donated but some on loan from our personal collections—were either missing in action, destroyed beyond repair, or snatched by the treasure seekers who travel in the wake of storms like this, tracking down valuables and taking advantage of other people's trauma.

I had no idea what to tell the kiddos.

Some things felt false. Others sounded dumb. There really wasn't anything to say. So we looked and wandered among the ruins. We gawked at the wondrous and obscene damage.

The hardest thing to accept, by far, was the toppling of a dozen, wizened walnuts trees. A few had already been sawed to pieces and hauled away. Some lay on the ground, partially amputated, looking as if they were just too tired to get up.

"*You* spend a century inching skyward and see how you feel when the wind blows down your life's work," the trees might have said if they could talk.

But they couldn't talk.

They had fallen . . . and they wouldn't get up.

Chapter 13

Glass House

Michelle

It's a glass house, Whetstone. The boys who live here are being watched all the time. Most of the time they need to stay within "eyesight and earshot," we say. That's why we have one staff for every three boys. Rarely do we make an exception.

It's a glass house for house parents, too. Good days and bad days are seen by all. And even if no one ever notices, you suspect they do.

As a house mom, I've had to focus on looking *out* of my windows, instead of assuming the world is looking *in* . . . and judging what it sees. In a glass house, you feel like you need to protect and guard yourself because you're on view all the time.

Ironically, on the day of the tornado, a newly hired house cleaner was scheduled to come to help me "get control" and "manage" my home at Whetstone. If the ranch house appeared more managed and less dirty, then I might feel less vulnerable and less stressed.

So what happens when the glass is shattered? When even the most transparent of barriers is taken away? When windows and doors are blown wide open, when boys leave, and traffic is backed up around the bend so people can drive by to gawk?

It is the Saturday morning after the tornado, and I am supposed to be teaching my Upward soccer players how to be more like Jesus. After all, I am the coach. But I am frazzled. On the way to the game, I am told that people are already at the ranch, cleaning up.

Without me?

I consider turning around.

Instead, I show up to the game a few minutes late, and as soon as I step out of the Suburban, I can feel the penetrating gaze of everyone there. They know about the tornado.

I am in a terrible mental state to coach kids' soccer. My six-year-old son Kellen, who has natural defensive skills, makes an incredible but illegal stop too close to the goal. The whistle blows. According to the Upward soccer rules of which I am unaware, he is not allowed to stop a ball that enters a large chalk semi-circle that functions as an imaginary goalie.

A penalty kick is awarded, and a point is scored. Kellen slouches toward me. His head is down; his eyes are teary.

I am crushed by the arbitrary cruelty of it all.

I feel as if my emotions might spin out of control.

This isn't the first time I've been surrounded by broken glass.

One year ago I was in a similar mental state. At that time, Ty and I lived in Phoenix, and I was unhappy. I'd had it. I needed something to change. I needed to change. Looking back, I recognize it as "divine discontent." God was stirring the pot.

In any case, my frustration culminated one morning in me smashing a mason jar on my kitchen floor. I'm not proud about it, but when your world is teetering on the edge, a nudge is all it takes for everything to fall to pieces.

"Hey God," I demanded. "Either make Arizona work, or take us back to Indiana where I grew up. We can't live like this anymore."

At the end of sweeping up, two large pieces remained, farther out and hidden from my initial view. This may sound crazy, but upon closer inspection, I promise you that their outlines actually resembled Arizona and Indiana.

That's just great, I thought. Even God is on the fence.

A few days later, my husband and I boarded a plane to attend a long-anticipated wedding in Arkansas. A friend of ours named Matt Foster was getting married.

It wasn't until we had boarded the plane and lifted off that Ty mentioned a short trip to see a boys ranch in Missouri.

Sometimes our worlds fall apart so that God can put them back together.

Chapter 14

IMAGERY

Matt

The wound is the place where the light enters you.
—Rumi
It's amazing what a man can see by the light of a burning bridge.
—George Straight

Sometimes you get so overwhelmed in the overcoming that you forget to appreciate the surviving.

I can't tell you how many times I've given this advice to others, but it was my wife, Jessica, who was the first person in the post-tornado chaos to help me follow it.

She did so by digging through the trash.

During a quick break from my frantic attempts to guide volunteer clean-up crews on Holy Saturday, I noticed Jessica from a distance. Almost one hundred volunteers had shown up that day, new ones rolling onto campus every hour, looking for ways to get involved. She strolled among them, lost in thought, picking around the edges of bustling activity.

Like most others, Jessica had hastily thrown on a tattered pair of mismatched clothes that wouldn't be any worse for the wear. Her straight blonde hair was tied back and tucked under an Arkansas baseball cap.

Eventually, she wandered over to a group of black garbage

bags. One at a time, she peeked into them and then, without warning, pulled out a beautiful but busted piece of oak trim, lifting it to the sky like Mary Poppins hoisting a lamp from her carpet bag. Jessica eyed it for a while, in a way that was bound to arouse question in anyone still enough to notice.

Why was she studying a broken piece of wood? It was trash, and we had a ton of it. I had been advising people all morning to pick this stuff up so we could keep moving.

I found myself staring at my wife in the same way she stared at the trash—curious, pondering, trying to appreciate the moment.

Suddenly, Jessica's blue eyes lit up, her head nodded in satisfaction, and with a familiar purse of her lips, she placed the hidden gem in a smaller bag she had at her side. From a distance our eyes met, and she called out a single word as she raised the bag in her hand:

"Imagery."

She walked around for a while that day—a Mary among scores of Marthas. She used her gift of attentiveness to collect memories which would be around long after the trash had been hauled off. If she would have opened the bag with you then, it would have told a story unto itself.

A broken clay planter, once teeming with life, now brimming with possibilities of what it might hold next.

A single sheet of music separated from its song, a love note once in hiding now open for all to see.

An old newsletter, found lying face up with an article entitled "Shelter from the Storm." Irony can be a strangely comforting thing.

Each of these things had new meaning. Fresh meaning. Meaning that meant even more.

Taking the time to look around, I saw even more possibility. Beautiful, old barn wood covered in faded red paint could be refashioned into gorgeous bookshelves, headboards, and cabinets. Fallen walnut trees which sheltered a home for decades could be transformed into a harvest table for thousands of family meals in years to come.

These would not be mere memories of an old life but harbingers of a new future.

That's what we do with grief when we do it well. We spend it balancing the memory of the past with our hope for the future. It's the tension between the two that provides the balance.

Don't get me wrong, there's something to be said for cleaning up life's messes. We were not made to live in them. While grief may be a good place to go, it is not a good place to stay. But too often, we try to get it all tidied up without taking the time to appreciate the fact that the mess didn't drown us.

So that afternoon, I took my cue from Jessica. I walked around for most of the day, basking in the love and support of a community that had dropped everything on its to-do list that beautiful spring day. I smiled and laughed and told stories.

There may have been some who begrudged my approach. But in the Bible, it's not Mary who gets rebuked. It's not the woman who took time to appreciate the moment when God showed up.

There would be plenty of time for me to clean later, but these hands and these feet would only be with me for so long.

Chapter 15

TARPS

Axel

We're trying to focus on the positive.

It is amazing that no one was killed. None of the ranch animals were even injured, all the way down to the lowliest of creatures—two pigs tucked almost cozily in a pocket beneath the collapsed barn.

The barn can be rebuilt.

So can the six-car garage swept from its concrete base, like the Whetstone boys sweep up a dust bunny during chore time.

And the shed which a group of volunteers from Kentucky helped us build just six months ago? Gone. Not a stick remains.

The roof can be replaced, although it is a total loss. And worse, water continues to leak down into the boys' bedroom, the living room, and eventually the schoolroom in the basement.

Moisture is our worst enemy at this point, so Brandon, our former house parent now-turned site director, works overtime to keep together the patchwork quilt of a half dozen different tarps. He has engineered them to drain out at roof's edge where we used to have a gutter. If we can't stop the leaking, more damage will occur in the sloppy aftermath than during the tornado strike.

But things have a way of drying out . . . eventually.

Windows, many of which have been blown out by the

tornado, along with their frames, can be ordered and reinstalled. The high winds sucked out a mattress, and it remains on the dirt road, several football fields away. Ripped open, the former bed reveals its springs, a gruesome image of what could have happened to one of our boys.

We'll get new mattresses.

We have no power and no plumbing. The ranch vehicles look like they've been in a demolition derby, and glass, well, glass is everywhere! It will take years before it all washes away.

But it will wash away, eventually.

We keep telling ourselves that we will be better, stronger, more equipped to aid others as they face the storms that drive them to our ranch.

That's what we keep telling ourselves.

But I'm not sure that's what Brandon is telling himself. He's too busy fixing stuff.

Brandon is naturally good at just about everything, which is great; but to be quite honest, it's a tad bit infuriating at times. The times when he beats me at frisbee golf, following his month-long hiatus from a sport I play every day, I'd say it's downright nauseating.

Seriously, now that I'm really thinking about it, Brandon makes me sick.

For example, Brandon built for his five kids a tree house that is like something from a Home Depot commercial—effortlessly constructed and perfectly proportioned. He finished off this wooden Taj Mahal with half-cut cedar logs to give it that "rustic" look. My tree house is rustic when it rolls out of bed in the morning. You'd think the guy has a degree in construction management or something. (*He does.*)

He's got a bag of tricks with cards, coins, paper clips, and folded paper that astounds the imagination. We sometimes joke that the two of us will collaborate on a coffee table book called *Brandon's Gadgets, Gimmicks, and Games* that will chronicle his many ice breakers. Look for it in stores at Christmas. It will sell a million copies.

Brandon and his wife, Laura, are committed to Dave Ramsey, envelopes, emergency funds, and saving for retirement. If that's not enough to make you hate the guy, I don't know what is.

His truck tires never seem to wear.

Brandon is a silky-smooth public speaker.

Brandon is never late for work. Did I mention he has five kids? How can you have five kids (with a sixth on the way), homeschool, and not be late for work. I mean, c'mon!

I sometimes think Brandon might be an alien, sent to this planet to investigate our species. He's trying to fit in by attempting to suck at all the things we suck at, but he sucks at sucking! He's too good.

It takes Brandon maybe two cups of coffee to install floor-to-ceiling kitchen shelves. I saw him do it with my own eyes. I'm talking a ten-foot ceiling. It would take me one month of Saturdays.

All of this makes it so unusual to see him struggling with those tarps on the roof of the ranch. Seriously, if Brandon can't do, it can't be done. It must be some Sisyphean task assigned to him by a spiteful deity as punishment for being so good at everything else.

You start to think like this in recovery. You might actually, with your very last drops of sweat and blood, get the rock to the top of hill. But what's the point? It's just going to roll back down.

One sunny afternoon a week or so after the tornado and in between rain bursts, I climbed up on the roof with Brandon. It was a good time to take a few photographs and to get a little perspective on the situation. It wasn't pretty. Two by fours lay higgledy-piggledy, nailed down in rough outline around the odd shapes formed by several contractor tarps that kept the house dry. You could see the wear and tear from the wind that kept ripping at the seams. It was driving him crazy because when the tarp didn't cover the damaged roof, water poured into the house and down through every level, causing havoc within.

To compound the problem, there was no reason to fix anything inside the house until the moisture issue was solved. These kinds of things kept our site director up at night.

On the positive side, they made for great pictures.

Brandon did not have the perfect upbringing. None of us do, but Brandon, like most of our residents, took the trials of childhood a little harder than most. He ended up drinking too much in college and fell in with the party crowd at a Christian university. (It's really not as hard as one might think.)

To his credit, he realized this before getting expelled and took drastic measures. He moved to Montana.

In Montana he grew a beard, donned flannel, picked up guitar, started listening to Chris Ledoux, learned to operate a chainsaw, and rented a small cabin in the woods within hitchhiking distance of Bozeman where he studied construction management at Montana State.

Brandon started reading his Bible. He started examining his unexamined life. Seeds were planted that eventually grew taller than the pines he cut down to pay for textbooks and tuition.

Two years after graduating and well into a successful career as a contractor, he felt dissatisfied. He couldn't imagine overseeing corporate construction and remodeling projects for the rest of his life. The pay was good, but the temptations facing a young man on the road could not be ignored for much longer. The rain, if it continued to fall, would eventually find its way to his soul.

So Brandon took the drastic step of calling up his old drinking buddy, and my cousin, Nate Dahlstrom.

After a few minutes of chitchat and a brief summary from Nate regarding the nascent idea of Whetstone Boys Ranch, Brandon cut right to the chase. "Nate," he said, "I'm in."

Just like that.

Though Whetstone was still just a concept on paper, their friendship helped sustained the dream for many years before it became a reality.

Once accepting the call, Brandon quit his high-paying job

and traded it in for volunteer work, alongside Jeremy, with troubled teens in Denver, Colorado.

Soon after, he met his wife, Laura, who was doing similar work in the Denver area. One year later, they married and moved to West Plains, Missouri, to open the site of Whetstone's first office, a shotgun style, 20 x 60 foot space off the town square, with a big glass window and a sign hanging out front.

It's the same sign that moved to Mountain View two years later, and three years after that was blown one mile down the road and salvaged by Ty and Michelle as they drove to the ranch on the night of the tornado.

On the roof that afternoon with Brandon, I point my camera down the long, winding road, which disappears around the bend. I take a few quick shots to capture the devastation, more apparent because the trees which would have hidden it are now gathered into piles of what look like cigarette butts.

I pan my camera back to a squatting Brandon, several nails pinched between his lips, swinging at the loose ends of a tarp.

He drives the remaining nails in smoothly, with the fewest hammer swings possible, then looks up and smiles at me as if to ask, "What can you do, Axel?"

Keep nailing, Brandon. Just keep nailing.

Chapter 16

EMPTY

Michelle

My Father's house has many rooms; if that were not so, would I have told you that I am going there to prepare a place for you? And if I go and prepare a place for you, I will come back and take you to be with me that you also may be where I am.
—John 14:3

It's a cool morning, and I want coffee. I can smell it coming from the ranch side, where someone else has started a pot. My *front door* actually opens into the ranch's main entryway, which has its own exit to the outside world. It's an odd set up, really. I can't exit my own living space without going through someone else's. And to make matters even more complicated, that someone else is often me. Both places are my home.

I walk over to the ranch side for a pick-me-up. It feels weird over here. Even though there is coffee, no one is around at the moment, and it's too quiet. The busyness that sometimes drives me crazy is gone, and I miss it.

My three sons aren't here because they're at our Peace Valley place with Ty. The ranch boys aren't here because they are, well, I don't know where they are. And I don't know when or if they will return. It's been weeks since the tornado, and we are still missing windows and a functional roof.

I am suddenly a mom without anyone to mother . . . in a house that is no longer a home.

As if to compound my existential crisis, my parents just signed closing papers on my childhood home of twenty years. And less than a week before the tornado hit Whetstone, Ty and I signed closing papers on a home in Peace Valley, fifteen minutes from the ranch. It was to be our getaway home.

But Whetstone would still be our main home.

Now, because of the tornado, everything has been turned upside down.

Suddenly, I think of the ranch boys. Ripped from their homes, deposited in a strange place, expected to make the best of it. I think that on many days, they do a better a job of coping than I do. We don't give them enough credit for this.

I will do better when they return.

I always set goals when we move into a new house. They are mental goals that I intend to keep first and foremost.

In this house, I'm not going to care how dirty the floors are.

In this house, I'm going to be full of love and grace.

Love, grace, *and* clean floors? Get real Michelle. This isn't a Swiffer commercial.

I like living at Whetstone. I really do. But I have to fight to make it *feel* like a home.

What I really need is for Jesus to go on before me, preparing it as only He can, so that when the boys come back in one month, or two, or three, it will be ready for whatever comes next.

Chapter 17

In the Dark

Matt

I'm writing in the dark now. It's been one month since the tornado, and we continue to struggle with power issues because of downed limbs and trees. I have a basement office, so I tend to leave the lights off anyway. I like working in the dark, but I usually have a choice in the matter.

I don't like working in the dark when I have no other option.

On the night of the storm, Brandon and I rendezvoused with Joey, Thomas, and the five boys huddled inside the pole barn, the only undamaged structure that remained. Earlier on the phone, Brandon and I had hatched a plan. During a five-minute call that I took in my underwear, we decided to retrieve the boys in a borrowed van and then transport them to Pomona Christian Church where they could catch some shut-eye for the night.

By the time we reached the ranch, the seven of them had been waiting for nearly two hours, trapped in a mix of delirium, exhaustion, and the excitement of a near-death experience. For the most part, they had little idea of the devastation that lay just outside the barn doors. They'd slithered over to the barn, a mere

150 yards away from the house, in the pitch-black dark, except for the tiny illumination of some headlamps. Along the way, they had passed a concrete slab that was once a shed, downed power lines, fallen trees, and loads of debris like garage siding, disc golf baskets, and splintered 2x4s.

In spite of all this, we found the boys in good spirits, a nervously giddy crew of sleep-deprived teenagers, mostly unaware of the enormity of what had just happened.

"Who has a test this morning?" I asked.

They looked confused.

"Well, whoever prayed to get out of school, kudos. It definitely worked." Kind of lame, but it broke the ice.

They spoke wide-eyed about the noises, about sitting down in the basement waiting for what seemed like nothing, and then hearing what one called a "monster throwing things around upstairs." They joked about how Mr. Liimatta would never let them leave school, and about how he'd still make them run this afternoon. Like always.

"Just dodge the carnage," one stoic impersonator said, in his best Liimattic voice.

"Tornados are no excuse for failing to make healthy decisions" said another, standing straight and rigid like Axel's known to do. They had obviously been having fun with this line of reasoning for quite a while. Humor can be a very helpful coping mechanism, so I let them have some fun.

However, at 3:30 a.m., the adrenaline started to wear off. The boys, along with their filters, were fading fast. Manufactured jokes at that time of the morning don't have happy endings. It was time to leave.

As we carefully drove away, I saw the zig-zagging flashlights of first responders poking around the house, revealing to me holes that shouldn't there. Yellow lights blinked at crazy angles, sifting through the wreckage of broken dreams, checking for who knows what. I imagined the worst and realized I wanted to be over there, too. I needed to know what we were up against.

Strangers were shedding light upon the situation while I was still very much in the dark.

IN THE DARK — MATT

The wind picks up outside my newly installed office window. The old one didn't necessarily break; it just busted open, allowing outside debris to cover the inside debris that normally covers my office floor.

Now I have a new window which, while more energy efficient and aesthetically pleasing, allows even less natural light than before. And I can't hear the glee of Michelle's children playing with the chickens above my head or riding around in their plastic John Deere. I can't listen to the pleasant patter of rain on those cold and wet November days when the sound reminds me of how good it feels to be dry.

It's one month after the tornado, and I'm still working in an eerie sort of darkness.

Chapter 18

SALVAGE

Axel

It would have been easy to just burn it all.

Push what was left of the old red barn into one giant pile and bonfire the heck out of it. That would have been the easiest thing to do.

Come to find out, insurance companies have rules against that kind of thing. But boy would that have felt good. To see it all go up in one giant cloud of smoke, reducing weeks' worth of back-breaking labor to a few hours. Our largest concern would be scorching the hotdogs we roasted on the flames.

No salvage work required.

If you've ever spent a day trying to rescue old wood, you know what I mean. You get splinters. You smack yourself in the shin with a crowbar. You accidentally pry wood into the softest parts of your body, getting stuck with a few rusty nails along the way for good measure.

You better wear goggles, or your focus will switch to salvaging what's left of your eye.

The good wood you have to move, stack, and protect from the elements while it cures. All of this takes time and money, energy and foresight. Most importantly, it takes patience.

In the same way, you can't rush the process of recovery.

You can't say to parents, "We'll have your boy back up and running in thirty days . . . or your money back." This explains the complete lack of infomercials aimed at struggling families with troubled boys.

Wow! This is not the same boy I sent to you on Monday. It's a miracle!

Incredible! The bad attitude is gone in just three easy applications!

You won't believe the results. Try it today! Call 1-800-NEW-BOYS. That number once again . . .

But this doesn't keep people from wanting it. If there were such a commercial, you can bet it would generate a lot of phone calls. Because people don't just want entertainment in thirty-second doses any more . . . they want social justice. They want Martin Luther-like Reformation in a twenty-four-hour news cycle.

All of which makes our job even harder. We're trying really hard to slow down in a culture that worships speed.

We're the little old lady driving in the left-hand lane.

Actually, my eighty-year-old mother-in-law travels faster than I do, so that might be a poor analogy. And besides, vehicular transport of any kind is way too fast to work as a metaphor for what we do. "*God doth not need / Either man's work or his own gifts,*" John Milton writes in "When I Consider How My Life is Spent."

> *. . . who best*
> *Bear his mild yoke, they serve him best. His state*
> *Is kingly; thousands at his bidding speed*
> *And post o'er land and ocean without rest:*
> *They also serve who only stand and wait.*
> —John Milton

I have a hard time being patient. At least Milton had a good excuse for his perceived lack of productivity. Blindness. Religious persecution. Political oppression.

Yet on a scale of 1 to 10, ranking "tendency to rush," I score in the triple digits. That's how bad I am at slowing down. I have what author John Ortberg calls "hurry-sickness." I'm that guy he describes as always seeing himself in relation to where he would have been if he had chosen the other checkout line. Indeed, I almost come to hate the jerk who walks out with his bag of carrots thirty-seven seconds before I do. Or the fellow traveler who shaves two minutes off his fifteen-hour trip to Michigan because he chose the left lane while going through Toledo.

Patience is a virtue, the old saying goes. And nowhere is this more true than in recovery.

You can't rip out crooked nails with brute force if you want to preserve the board.

Chapter 19

Garden Variety

Michelle

"Mom, W— is at it again," my son Kellen yells from our guest room.

There is a tornado in the garden.

This tornado carries a stick or metal rod. I'm not quite sure, but I think it is some tool I am supposed to have locked up.

"Mom, he's in the tomatoes."

Sure enough, I look out the window in time to see W— hacking away at our tomatoes.

I love tomatoes. I love the variety of their red hues and the rich, earthy smell when they are freshly picked. I love cutting them into juicy slices, canning them, and freezing them. I had big plans for those tomatoes.

But the human tornado has other plans. He beats my dreams and my tomato plants to the ground.

W—'s outburst has come on the heels of many other temper tantrums during which I have felt the need to lock my kids up on our side of the house to keep them safe. These periods of turbulence are relatively rare at the ranch, but when they happen, I'm quickly reminded that this is a *therapeutic* boarding school.

As a mom, my heart aches for W—'s mom because this has been her everyday tornado. The potential for collateral damage has driven her to take drastic measures to protect her boy, her family, and her marriage. She has sent her son across the country to get the help he needs, the help which she feels is *her* duty. She has guilt for letting it get to this point, guilt for letting him stay too long, guilt for letting him go.

On this morning, my sympathy for this mom moves to empathy because I'm feeling the same thing. It's becoming increasingly clear that Whetstone isn't going to be the right place for W——. This is not his first outburst by any measure.

And even though it's not my fault, I feel like I have failed him. He's here because we said we could help.

As it turns out, he won't let us.

It is one year later, and this boy's mom has arrived to help us with the tornado clean-up.

The tornado has struck right in the middle of planting season, the time when I dream of tomatoes and a bountiful garden. We have seeds that need to be set down.

It feels strange planting without any boys in the house to feed, but we bury the seeds in faith, trusting that God will return boys back to Whetstone.

All by herself, with whining chainsaws and groaning tractors all around her, this mom plants our garden. It is the same plot her son wrecked the summer before. We are all aware of the irony. *The tragic and redemptive beauty of a mother, on her knees, sowing seeds to help a ranch that couldn't help her boy.*

By faith she plants our garden, hoping that boys will return to Whetstone and hoping that her own boy will return to her someday.

Chapter 20

AROMA

Matt

My office smells fantastic. That hasn't always been the case. In fact, between my organizational ineptitude, sweaty teenage boys, my ever-diminishing desire to clean, and a gift for ignoring things, my office has rarely seen better days—a sad truth since it was merely an unfinished concrete box in a basement before my arrival.

Cleanliness is not my forte.

But if we dig deeper, as is my wont, I'm actually quite good at cleaning and organizing—maybe too good. My type of cleaning is so exhaustingly thorough that it leaves me too tired to do it again, and when the inevitable need comes round once again, the haunting memory is far too fresh to allow me to re-victimize myself in such a way.

So actually, my untidiness is more about self-care than anything else.

How's that for self-analysis?

I obviously love justifications. In fact, I've become so comfortable with them that I can justify my justifications. Meta-justification, if you will.

Like I said, my office smells fantastic. But up until a couple of days ago, it still had debris strewn across the floor, remnants of the great "tor-Mado" as young Kellen, one of Michelle's sons, calls it.

It's mid-June, and the storm is two months passed; but just last week, Kellen and I had a cleaning party where we put on our "meticulous glasses" and vacuumed every tiny sliver of glass and straw that remained.

It's not like we moved furniture and found my second cousin who had been missing since that ugly family reunion in Tupelo, but there was a spider that had passed an entire lifetime in a comfortable, undisturbed home before we vacuumed up his long-dead body.

In the interest of full disclosure, during my single days when I lived in Searcy, Arkansas, a tree frog made his way through the shower drain and took up residence on the clear vinyl shower curtain. He inhabited my bathroom for so long I gave him a name and greeted him each morning before I showered. (If that story doesn't give you a deep appreciation for my wife and what she puts up with, then nothing will. Or, you might be like one of my close friends who declared he had "no more room for the amazement.") Eric the Frog stayed for six days. I told the doubters it was therapeutic for me to leave him there, you know, to help me overcome my fear of frogs. That's not entirely false, and I can still make a strong case for it. Yet, if we move past the meta-justification and get down to the nitty gritty, I wasn't becoming more comfortable with the frog being there, I was just getting better at ignoring him.

While this may not be the best practice in my personal life, it's not a bad trait to have as a counselor. I have to be okay with sitting in a mess and not letting it overwhelm me. It's a necessary quality when walking with families through their darkest and dirtiest places. There's usually a fair amount of crap to deal with.

My office is in the basement of the house parents' side of the ranch.

To enter it, a visitor must step up and over a threshold, then through a small waiting area decorated in a loosely western motif. The wireless internet doesn't often make it this far. Suffice it to say, I have a literal and figurative separation from the rest of the ranch. The boys don't, can't, and must not know everything that happens in this office. Some of this stems from the need for confidentiality, but even without this ethical bind, there's really no need to spread their garbage around. The ranch needs a messy place. And my office just happens to be particularly well suited to the task.

To use another metaphor, if Whetstone were an old sailing vessel, my office would represent the compartments in the hull below the surface of the water. Whenever we start taking on water, we just seal them off, one at a time, so that the rest of the ship doesn't go down with it. I know my fellow friends and coworkers wouldn't intentionally leave me down here to die, but that doesn't keep me from feeling like they might forget.

Like a ship tossed about at sea, many of our boys find themselves tossed about, too. And on that stray ship, there comes a time when septic things must be dealt with—literally and figuratively. The crap that has entered their world, by choice or circumstance, needs to find its way out. (Please forgive any crudeness on my part, but trust me. I'm going somewhere with this.)

Sometimes it's the tar-like newborn poop that you can't get off anything no matter how hard you try. Other times, it's just your garden-variety bull crap.

Regardless, when the clothing of action is removed and the soul stands exposed, it's not a place you enter with ease or carelessness. That, I believe, is why there is such a reverence when others cross the threshold and knock on my office door.

I used to think it was from fear of flying feces that folks would crack the door slowly, coming in with turned faces, listening ears in the lead. I've come to learn, however, that their timidity is more like that of Moses approaching the burning bush. The flickering light beneath the door makes them both curious and hesitant to discover what lies beyond.

It's a holy place where things are laid bare.

So maybe, instead of wearing my boots with jeans tucked in during such moments, I should take them off and go barefoot.

… Chapter 21

INCREMENTALISM

Axel

Change happens gradually over time . . . except when it happens all at once, which it does . . . sometimes.
 Ipso facto.
Being in the path of a tornado results in certain changes that occur within seconds and others that take years to process and fathom.

Like trauma and addiction.
Like recovery and reconciliation.
Like falling in and out of love.
Like growing up. Like getting old. These are not overnight affairs.

The theory of incrementalism—yes, it has its own page on Wikipedia so it's a thing—is that organizations are better served with long-range planning that focuses more on the importance of learning from our mistakes than on wasting energy trying to avoid them. Mistakes will be made. That's pretty much the only thing we know for sure. So let's plan on it.

In essence, your long-range plan should be to resist the temptation to plan long range.

Incrementalism is alive and well here at Whetstone Boys Ranch. In fact, it comforts me to know a formal theory exists that describes our approach. Our lack of a system at times can actually be systematic. (Ahhh. I for one will sleep better knowing this.)

Chipping away at our ridiculously long post-tornado to-do list is like chipping away at the thick, translucent epoxy of shame, guilt, fear, and insecurity that covers our boys from head to toe. Many of them look just fine. We find the cracks.

That tapping sound you hear around this place? It's not just the plumber fixing a leak, or the cabinet guy remodeling our pantry.

It's Whetstone.

It's the tension that we all live with. It's iron sharpening iron.

You can't just peel off layers of shellac like you peel the skin off an orange.

Some of it might never come off. And what does come off will take several layers of skin with it.

So we tap. And chisel. And sand with fine-grit paper.

We learn to crawl before we walk. Walk before we run.

We take things slowly even when our instincts tell us to push the pedal.

It's why the Marines, not known for their patience, like to say, "*Slow is steady. Steady is smooth. Smooth is fast.*"

It's one of those paradoxes we're so fond of around here. It's why we use paradoxes. Because they take time to sink in.

And that's one thing we have to our advantage with our boys when they return. Time is on our side. We can make it drip if we want to. Not in a Chinese-water-torture kind of way, but in a Thomas-Merton-breathe-and-get-to-the-bottom-of-things kind of way.

Incrementalism was introduced to the world in a 1959 article titled, "The Science of Muddling Through," by Yale University economist Charles Lindblom.

I really wish we still called it that.

Chapter 22

HORSES

Michelle

Since I was a little girl, I've had a romanticized but deeply disappointing relationship with horses.

It all started with two horses I grew up with on my parents' farm. Ponies actually. Blaze and Beauty were their names, and boy, did I have high hopes for them.

For the most part, I enjoyed the responsibility of cleaning their stall. It gave me an opportunity to dream I was someone else, someone I really felt I was deep down inside. I rode the bus to school every day reading book after book of the Thoroughbred Series. I pictured myself all grown up, working with horses for a living—a reverie which helped pass the time.

The reality is that my younger sister was tremendously better with our horses, moving with ease between walk, trot, and gallop. I, on the other hand, found myself lying on the ground routinely, tears streaming down my face, struggling with the indignity of being told again and again to "get back on the horse."

It should come naturally.
I shouldn't need so much help.

A brief look at my family credentials would seem to indicate I was born in a saddle. Not so. I'm just a big, scared girl with high hopes.

Flashback to 2004, at Timothy Hill Children's Ranch, on a date with Ty . . . on horseback. I'm thankful he'd already asked me to be his wife at this point—a fact which prevented a total meltdown during the special moment we were about to endure.

I'm sure I looked good getting on the horse. I've always been good at that part.

I saddled the horse by myself, cinch strap and all. No help from Ty needed. And the next part was my favorite. Foot in stirrup, swing the other leg around, and look awesome doing it.

Everything after that came straight out of a bad romantic comedy.

I told the horse to go left. It went right.

I told it to go right. It went left.

I said "Whoa!" It must have heard "Go!"

I couldn't even stop it from running back to the barn, a cardinal sin of which I am fully aware. You should hear my grandma talk about how *we* never let the horse run back to the barn.

Of course, on this day, my horse insisted. I promise, I couldn't do a thing to stop it.

Meanwhile, Ty coached me, giving me encouraging instruction. He reminded me to stay calm and take control. He was a good fiancé.

Now, after all these years, with three boys and a farm of my own, it still feels like something I should be able to do.

All moms feel this way on some level.

It should come naturally.

I shouldn't need so much help.

And if you're a Whetstone mom, you have a double dose of anxiety, and second guessing, and insecurity about how well you're riding, and about what people think of you when you fall off the horse. In my experience, everyone seems to have an opinion about what you should do, where you should go, how you should turn, how you should stop, and so on, and so forth.

I can't even imagine what the moms of our five absent ranch boys are going through right now.

Broken down, face in the dirt, we moms are smacked with our own insecurities, difficulties, and weaknesses. But if we're in a family that loves us, we know that everyone wants us to get back on and try again. They don't care how many times we've fallen off. They really don't.

They just want us along for the ride.

Chapter 23

STU

Matt

I love baby animals.

Human offspring are neat and all, but they require too much patience. Baby animals are up and at 'em, right away. They don't spend a lot of time crying and fussing. They get straight to the living.

So every day in the spring, I drive more slowly to work, hoping to catch a glimpse of new life trotting through the woods and open fields. Wood ducklings jumping out of trees, little poults awkwardly running behind the mother hen, tiny rabbits scurrying in all directions.

My wife and I live far enough out in the country to see plenty of action. Many days, I'm the only one driving some of these roads until the mailman comes much later in the day.

The swath of destruction left by the tornado made my animal watching even easier.

It was on one such occasion, several weeks after the tornado, that I sensed the telltale sign of a baby deer—those beautiful and unmistakable white spots—not off in the woods or field but on the side of the road like trash left behind in the wake of the road grader. They were only in the corner of my eye, but I knew immediately what they meant.

The orphaned fawn wasn't balled up like you normally find fawns at that time of year, staying low and hoping nothing sees them until mom gets back. He had his front right hoof draped over his neck in a way that would make contortionists cringe, and the look in his eye wasn't the normal, wide-eyed, trying-to-be-still, and hoping-you-don't-notice-me kind of look. It was "I've made it this far, and this as far as it gets." I know the one. I see it in our boys' faces. And in their parents' faces when they deliver their young to our doorstep.

From inside my truck, I stared at the fawn for a bit, trying to figure out how much longer he would make it. I really thought he might expire at any moment.

When it became apparent he wouldn't, I exited the cab and inched my way towards him. He didn't even flinch. Once beside him, I untangled his leg from behind his head and moved him from one side of the road to the other and into the woods where there was a slight chance his mother might be waiting for him. But there were no snorts or blows, and when I set him down, he did not scamper, stumble, or make any attempt to move or hide. He just crumbled, heavy beneath the burden of what this world had to offer. To keep on going was not an option.

Feeling as if I had no other option, I loaded him gently into the back of my truck. I would be the Good Samaritan this time. I would not pass by on the other side of the road or pretend I didn't notice his plight.

I wasn't aware of many things when I first signed on as deer caretaker. (My wife points out that this is a trend in my life.) You just assume that animals know how to do things. You take it for granted. Like the time that I adopted a wild mustang from the government; you take for granted that a horse has seen fences and that it's halter broken. Not so, I found out many bruises later.

We named our baby deer Vincent Stewart Gary Frick Jr., or "Stu" for short.

Slowly but surely, Stu worked his way into my family's

heart. He stumbled back and forth at odd angles as he learned to coordinate his many joints and nursed from a bottle as if he were born to do so. Surprisingly, and against all odds, we discovered that Stu was a cuddler.

I was told that raising a deer was great preparation for having a child, pushing aside the fact that it's illegal, I guess. And I wish that were the case because it would mean my newborn child will only require five short feedings each day; and afterwards, they will wander off to bed themselves down in the tall grass where they'll sleep peacefully until the next appointed feeding.

Eventually, I called Stu by name at feeding time, prompting him to slowly rise from his slumber, wobble his way into a concentrated walk and then a quick stride towards his next meal. He wasn't a very picky eater, attacking the bottle like it needed convincing. At the 5 p.m. and 10 p.m. feedings, he worked himself straight into a snooze. So, if I played my cards right, I got about fifteen to twenty minutes of good cuddling.

It was in those semi-conscious moments that we watched hunting shows on TV. Partly because he needed to know early on that there were people like that in this cruel, cruel world, and no deer of mine would be sent out there uninformed—and partly for the irony.

I fed Stu in my lap on the way to work each morning, always passing the point where I first rescued him. After arriving at Whetstone with a full stomach, Stu would unfold himself from the truck cab and then walk twenty-five yards over to the tall grass where he'd bed down until midday.

He was rarely vocal, but when he was, it was usually at lunch. Everyone from boys to contractors to volunteers enjoyed holding my little Stu while he sucked down his little baby bottle during the lunch break. He was a great distraction for me and for many others who paused to take pictures with the baby fawn and forget we were rebuilding after a tornado.

I'd call his name again at the end of the workday, bottle in hand, and he'd come hobbling along as best his little legs would let him. This was the first sign that something wasn't quite right.

As it turns out, my Stu was developing scabs on the front

of his knees from bedding down. With no mother to attend in nature's way to the cause of this seemingly minor problem, his knees got a pretty serious infection. In the end, this turned out to be the thing that did him in—a knee infection.

Vincent Stewart Gary Frick, Jr., lived from May 26th to June 28th, 2015. He was a frustratingly welcome addition to my life in a time when I needed something to nurture and lift my spirits. Maybe it was cosmic irony that he left this world just days after our first boy arrived back on campus . . . I don't know. I just know I liked hanging out with him.

So now every time I see a three-month-old fawn running behind its mother, capable of keeping pace and feeding itself, I'm angry that it's not Stu. That should be my little guy, running free, frolicking in the field, and coming back to check in on occasion.

I'd love to be able to tell you that I am grateful for the time that we had together, and that he was a blessing if even for a short time. I'd love to tell you that I learned valuable lessons about nature and myself, and in time I might.

But right now it really just hurts that he's not here, and I guess that's all it needs to be.

Chapter 24

BIG BOY

Axel

Jeremy Thompson is my oldest and closest friend. He is also my boss.

How these two things coexist is an interesting tale . . . one that starts way back in 1974. (Cue the *Wayne's World* flashback music . . . *doodle-eeyu, doodle-eeyu.*)

Jeremy Thompson was born on July 18, 1974, forty-seven days after and about ten miles from where I entered the world. His parents knew my parents. They doubledated in college. Like me, he was a firstborn child and firstborn grandchild. His father also served in the Army during Vietnam. We attended the same church while growing up.

But that's where the similarities stop.

Beyond these facts, we had very little in common.

If I was Jacob, he was Esau. Linked together from birth, but about as different as Detroit and Damascus.

As a hunter and outdoorsman, he liked to shoot things. As an urban dweller who grew up in gang territory, I preferred not getting shot at.

As a country boy, he was attracted to simple truths. As a city boy, I thrived on modern dilemmas.

In temperament, he is choleric and submitted without fight to a serious case of senioritis beginning in his junior year of high school. I am sanguine and over-committed to opportunities provided in the classroom and on the court. I was a three-sport varsity athlete. A straight-A student. I was in the Key Club, the Chess Club, the Drama Club, the Bowling Club. If it had enough people to be called a club, I considered joining it.

Jeremy's favorite extracurricular activity besides soccer (he was an exceptional defenseman who played with prodigious tenacity and endurance) was showing up to school early and watching people park their cars. He loved to rate them. Low scores were given for bad angles, awkward approaches, and indecisiveness.

At the end of our respective high school careers, Jeremy headed off to Alpena Community College in northern Michigan near his ailing grandparents whom he helped support. He hunted deer in the fall and fished for steelhead in the spring. Here, he earned an associate degree in concrete technology, with honors.

I chose to attend the United States Military Academy at West Point. My intentions were to pursue a career in politics and someday be elected to high office. That was the plan in the spring of 1992.

(Did I mention that Jeremy is now my boss?)

As I've already explained, West Point necessitated a course correction. I returned home after two life-changing months and attended Michigan Christian College for my freshman year. I eventually finished my collegiate career at Harding University in Arkansas. I married a girl from Tennessee, became a teacher, moved to Kentucky in 2000, started a family, and bought a dream home in the bluegrass countryside. I settled down there as an AP English teacher and debate coach at Henry Clay High School in Lexington, with plans to retire at the ripe old age of fifty-five and travel the world in ways George Bailey could only dream.

Jeremy completed his concrete management degree then acquired a bachelor's in construction management at Ferris State in Big Rapids, Michigan. (Near the top of his class, in both cases, I will add.) Our paths crossed again at Harding University for what you might consider a "gap year," during which he unsuccessfully attempted to find a wife. He accepted a job with construction giant Pulte Homes in 1997, developed a mysterious life-threatening growth on his brain stem within six months of accepting the position, almost died, and suffered through a decade of chemotherapy and steroid treatments. During his recovery, he met my cousin Nate who had a dream of starting a boys ranch. Jeremy moved to Colorado to volunteer, along with Brandon, at a nonprofit that served homeless teenagers in downtown Denver, spent a summer at Timothy Hill Children's Ranch, married a girl from Texas, and then moved to Missouri where he knew a guy who knew a guy who might just have a piece of land for sale.

All during this time (I found out later), my wife, Christine, had been artfully employing a Whetstone coffee mug designed for an early Whetstone fund-raising campaign.

"Would you like cream with that coffee?" she might say, flipping her long brown hair and turning the mug ever so slightly so that the WBR logo faced me directly before pouring the delicious nectar into my ready cup.

"How about some hot chocolate?" she'd ask during a movie while a nice fire crackled beside us. Out would come the WBR mug, its stark black letters contrasting sharply on the smooth, white, ceramic exterior.

Star of two dozen plays, and a talented artist gifted in creative expression of all sorts, my wife knows the value of a well-placed prop or grace note. It's what first drew me towards her and continues to do so after twenty-five years of marriage.

The little things are the big things.

Because of Christine's encouragement (subliminal and otherwise), we moved to West Plains, Missouri, where an English teacher/debate coach position had opened just hours before I waltzed in from Kentucky to inquire about a job. That's a story for another time, but we were certain that God had spoken to us in a way that could not be misunderstood.

Meanwhile, the 37th Judicial Circuit Court of Missouri (the one represented in the film *Winter's Bone*) hired Jeremy as a juvenile officer, and a local elementary school employed his wife. So voila! We became "Show-Me State" neighbors at the age of thirty-six. This in itself is a small miracle.

In the spring of 2011, we both resigned from our day jobs and joined Brandon Maxwell as full-time, salaried employees of a ranch that still did not exist, except in the abstract as a 501(c)(3) nonprofit.

In the three months that followed, we raised $100,000 and closed on a 10,000 square foot home, along with 285 acres. This was during the housing crisis, mind you.

Slightly before all of this happened, my cousin Nate's life took a different path, so we shuffled roles. Brandon and his wife Laura become Whetstone's first house parents. I became the headmaster/teacher of our school. And Jeremy became, of all things, the executive director, aka my boss!

In another strange twist, it was my father (the one with the space helmet) who warned Jeremy about praying that the Lord's will be done in his life. My dad cautioned him about becoming an instrument of divine providence, a piece of clay on a potter's wheel. It was prayer such as this that led my father to joining the Special Forces.

Over breakfast at a Big Boy Restaurant in the summer of 1997, my dad told Jeremy, straight up.

"That's a dangerous prayer."

Jeremy prayed it anyway. One month later, he was diagnosed with an inoperable brain tumor.

If that's how God treats his friends, I, for one, would hate to be his enemy. But as I say, my dad also had prayed that prayer. He'd visited the "house of mourning" and emerged a wiser man.

And it is this, at the end of a very long day of working with boys whose needs despite all my best efforts remain unmet, that allows me to trust my boss, Jeremy Thompson.

We don't run a House of Mirth, like the coachman in *Pinocchio* who lures lost boys to Pleasure Island. And despite our best intentions, Whetstone is not a "very, very nice house." As for the boys, they may look good on the surface and, like my dad, be a barrel of laughs. But underneath, they are broken bones and busted dreams. They are at their wits' end.

But if the Bible is correct, that might just be the best place for them and for us.

Like Daniel in the den, Joseph in the pit, and Jonah in the whale, Whetstone's executive director has been there. Jeremy's faced a few storms already, and he's seen Jesus emerge from the stern of the boat to quiet the wind and waves.

Chapter 25

Buried Alive

Michelle

Will someone please tell me why we're doing a deep clean today?

We're still hanging and sanding drywall. I thought it was common knowledge that you can't do a deep clean before you sand dry wall.

The house doesn't feel anywhere close to ready, and our first boy to return post-tornado arrives in just a few days.

I know everything can't be perfect, but I'm swamped. The ninety-nine packages of ground beef in the freezer offer no comfort at this point. The tornado didn't actually kill our cows, but it did do a number on our fences. And no fences equals no cows, which makes me sad because it's another reminder that we're not ready to be a boys ranch yet.

And while we're at it, why did anyone think I'd want a cow cut into ninety-nine packages of ground beef? Tenderloin would have been nice. How about some steak? Steak is good. But no one thought to ask me. Just throw it all into the grinder, they thought. The house mom will just have to work with whatever squeezes out. I know I sound bitter, but it's really hard to be hopeful right now. I'm settling for honest.

I actually have ninety-eight packages because I gave one to the Coats, the dear couple who has managed our garden since we opened in 2011. At least we'll have vegetables to feed our first returning resident.

I know I need to trust it's all going to be okay. Take things one day at a time. And whenever our first boy gets here, I just have to make good food and be nice. That's not too hard, is it?

But the timing of this feels like another disaster. I'm not ready. I can't handle any more turbulence.

Right now I just ache, buried beneath the stuff piled up on our side of the house. And I'm wondering if anyone has bothered to notice.

Chapter 26

Country Roads

Matt

When we had boys living here, we would usually end each school day in a flurry of activity to finish goals, hand in assignments, and convert the school from an academic space to a recreational room for the evening. The boys would then hurry up four flights of stairs to change clothes, so they could be back on ground level in time to run two miles—rain, snow, sleet, or shine.

I don't know if anyone else finds it ironic, but we built an entire program dedicated to training skilled "runners" how to run. They run from their past. And now, they run from Axel, who usually starts last so he gets a good view of everyone. Woe is the boy who tries to stop for a breather on these jaunts.

For many years friends and colleagues have noted my disdain for running. I was a pitcher in my brief high school baseball experience because there was less running. I was the lead-off batter in city league softball because all I had to do was get on base. I could slap some Texas-league single over the middle infield and saunter to first if I had to, but nothing is better for the psychological edge than to be given that base for free simply because the pitcher was too inept to deliver enough strikes to make me swing. I'm not above charity.

That is not to say I can't run or that I'm not fast. I can hold my own. I just don't want to. It's like washing the dishes or doing the taxes: I'm capable, but I'd much rather let someone else do it.

By contrast Axel, in pied-piper-like fashion, has led his merry band of runners up and down the same dirt roads since the day Whetstone received its first boy in the fall of 2011. And outside of a few futile attempts to prove that I've "still got it," I've just let them go.

Yes, there are the occasional slow-goers, the new guys who haven't quite bought in yet, or the tough days when someone really isn't "feeling it." But the vast majority of the time, our guys are out there busting it, trying to beat their own best time.

I'm not sure why the running started. It may be because we are just outside of West Plains, Missouri, which is home to Missouri Sports Hall of Fame coach, Joe Bill Dixon, who is also a former Whetstone board member. Or it may be because it's something Axel's good at, and he wants to share it with them.

Either way, Axel is a genius. Think about it. He has scheduled an activity that allows him to get paid while doing his daily run, and he has somehow convinced a bunch of incalcitrant teenage males (most of whom have little previous running experience) to join him.

If Axel were writing this, he'd probably tell you how rewarding it is to see the changes that occur inside and out, how the boys become stronger and more confident as they succeed and grow. He'd explain that running boosts endorphins, reduces stress, fights depression, and improves sleep. He'd talk about how the boys who finish first will cheer for the new guy that struggles up the driveway to finish gasping on the front steps. He no doubt basks in the smiles, high fives, and fist bumps after a boy beats his old record time, relishing the sweaty, odor-wrought hugs to celebrate such occasions.

But none of that explains why I love the running program.

I love the symbolism.

As I mentioned earlier, we've got a house full of runners.

They may have little to no experience with running as a sport, or an exercise, or even as a mode of transportation, but all of my guys have been running for a long time—and they're good at it.

For various reasons and with varying degrees of self-awareness, they have chosen the escape route. Deep hurts. Traumatic experiences. In one way or another, they've fled to find some peace in the chaos. Others have stress, intensity, and expectations which seem too much to bear, so instead of being blown away they've tried to outrun the wind.

Others just don't want to face the responsibility and, for many different reasons both good and bad, don't stick around to see it through.

And now this. A tornado has them on the run again. An actual tornado.

So today, I find myself looking down the country road that our boys used to dust up at 3:30 in the afternoon. I squint to see their bobbing heads on the horizon, their bright yellow t-shirts inching towards me . . . some sign of hope they are coming back.

COMFORT

"What Kind of Man Is This?"

What kind of man is this? Even the winds and the waves obey him!

MATTHEW 8:26

Chapter 27

PROOF

M— (a resident during the night of the tornado)

Three nights after returning home, I snuck out, met up with some friends, hotboxed one of their parent's cars, and by two o'clock could barely walk home.

Within the first week, the police picked me up and fined me two-hundred dollars for trespassing as well as possession of an illegal substance and drug paraphernalia. Let's just say I hadn't yet learned my lesson.

Things continued along these lines for the two months I was at home after the tornado. It was one bad decision after another. I avoided the root of my problems and perpetuated the unending and all-too-familiar power struggles with my parents.

And then the call came that the ranch would reopen. I would be one of the few boys going back. Whoopee.

My friends decided to throw a going-away party for me with predictable results. I ended up hungover and even more miserable that I had to return to Whetstone. Nothing I said or did would convince my parents to keep me at home. In fact, everything I said and did had the opposite effect. I was a wreck. The only consolation was that I would be spending one week at family camp in Alabama before returning. Normally, I wouldn't have been too excited about Bible camp, but compared to the alternative it seemed okay.

It sounds corny, but I was on my knees after the second sermon. No joke.

I can't explain it, but I found myself on the ground, asking, no, *begging* God to reveal Himself to me in a real way. I told Him I didn't want a blind faith. I wanted more. I needed some sort of revelation.

In front of the large crowd, I felt like an infected wound whose bandage has just been ripped off, but I didn't care. The pressure was too great. I couldn't hide it anymore.

Thankfully, the minister stepped down from the pulpit and sat beside me. He put his arm around me and then asked, gently, if he could pray for me.

Yes, I said. I needed emotional and physical healing. I needed proof.

As he prayed in his soft preacher voice, I started to feel something new. It was unlike anything I expected to feel or anything I had ever felt before. But something big started to happen.

Something told me that the proof I was looking for wouldn't come from complete healing. Many people suffer like me. Suffering doesn't disprove God's existence any more than a lack of suffering proves it.

In that moment, the one which may have never come without a tornado that forced me to spin out of control, God opened my eyes. He showed me that He had a plan for me, whether I knew it or not.

I wept.

Right there in front of all those strangers in Alabama. It was one of those uncontrollable tear storms with snot bubbles and everything.

After several minutes, I was exhausted. And still. I heard the blood pumping in my ears. I felt new, like I could start over.

I had heard other people talk about a great weight being lifted in moments like this, but now I understood what they meant. The sadness and anger I had been carrying around was gone.

In its place was the happiness and relief of a lost child who had just found his father.

And then, a funny thing happened. I started smiling. Like the crying, it was uncontrollable. I must have looked pretty goofy up there at the front of the chapel. A few minutes earlier I would have choked down the emotions and stayed cool, but now I didn't care.

I grew up in a religious family, but I'm new to my personal walk with God. I am still in the process of figuring out what this means. I'm back at Whetstone Boys Ranch with a new take on life.

I don't think God would cause a tornado to hit the ranch, but who knows? All I know is that He took the opportunity to work in my life, and I'm glad for it.

You can draw your own conclusions.

Chapter 28

YEAST

Axel

Three of the five boys with us during the tornado will not return. Predictably, we're getting mixed reviews. It's not like any of them were ready to go home.

Also predictable, upon hearing about relapses and regressions, is the examination of what we could have done differently. When this happens to any former resident, it's hard to brush aside the feeling that all the work we did together was a waste.

Even if we know it wasn't.

We know that seeds planted during their time with us may take a lifetime, or a generation, to grow.

We also know that God designed us with a will—these boys have stubborn streaks that make DiMaggio's 56-gamer look weak—and that only He can change the heart.

With years of professional training and personal experience, we have learned to distance ourselves from the train wreck of aftercare breakdowns and the collateral damage that occurs when a speeding hunk of human steel comes hurling off the track.

We do not doubt our calling or get pitched into despair over things we can't control. We don't make bargains with chaos. Not when we have our business hats on that is. (Let's leave our personal lives out of this, thank you.)

And we'll not pretend that our "success rate," whatever that means, is the gold standard. Not at this point, at least.

The tornado makes me think I don't know a whole heckuva lot about anything. Least of all, the human heart, which is a tornado all unto itself, ever swirling in a "glass cage of emotion," to toss in a Will Ferrell quote.

And there I go again: punctuating my hurt feelings with humor, distancing myself from the pain of disappointment, and pretending that it doesn't matter too much to me when I hear a former graduate is back doing _____.

That's what happened this morning.

He's back doing _____? Are you kidding me? After all the work we did together? After all the sacrifices his parents made to keep him here? After all the love he received, and counseling, and interaction with nature, and academic mentoring, and good food, and exercise.

He chooses _____ after all that?

I really don't get this whole God's providence thing. And to be honest, it's God I end up getting mad at if I think about it long enough.

Why do You let Your children drown in pools of their own filth? Why do you let us return like dogs to our own vomit?

It sure makes it hard on us down here to justify You up there.

And then it hits me.

I'm more concerned about how it makes me look when a boy fails. He represents me. He has been branded whether he likes it or not with W-B-R.

When he fails, I fail. Because of my selfish human nature, this hurts much more than the vicarious pain I feel for him or his family.

So stop reading right now, and say a prayer for me. Ask God to soften my heart, to wound my pride.

Jesus said, "Beware the yeast of the Pharisees." He was speaking to me. Warning me to avoid the greatest of all sins, the unforgiveable sin, committed only by those 'holy' enough to be in a position to commit it.

Blaspheming the Holy Spirit.

I once heard a story of a man who lived in terror at the thought that he had committed this sin by joking that God would open up the roof of a church building, like Texas Stadium, and glide on down for a visit. He was being facetious about how this church viewed itself as having 5G connection with God while the rest of us were still on 3G. Point is, he felt bad afterwards. "Going to hell" bad.

Now I'd certainly tell this man that God can take a joke. He isn't waiting to pounce on us after each off-hand remark.

But I think the joking man may have been on to a little something. He had put himself in God's place. Judging the quick and the dead. Only God can do that. And if you think you're good enough to do all that, you're good enough to save yourself and raise your own dead body from the grave.

That's true blasphemy.

You don't come back from that.

Chapter 29

FORKS, PT.1

Michelle

To a newcomer, the Whetstone house can be a bit disorienting. As I've explained earlier, it's really two homes in one, cordoned off to meet the minimum standards of privacy for all involved.

There is the house parents' side, a 1950s style, two-story brick home encompassing about 3,000 square feet. Then there is what we call the "ranch side," which was converted from a 7,000 square foot dormitory-style vacation home added on in the early 90s. The two houses are separated by a single door accessed from the front entryway—a door, in fact, which sits at the bottom of a flight of stairs leading up to the boys' bedrooms. Simply put, one cannot enter the house parents' side without entering the ranch side first.

There is really no way to keep everything family-only on *our* side or ranch-only on the ranch side. Boundaries are a constant struggle. So imagine how these lines might blur even further when Ty and I host a small group Bible Study at the ranch on our "night off."

In theory, small groups provide Christians the opportunity

for real fellowship—praise, worship, and study together. They also, in theory, allow all group members an opportunity to be open about their lives, without having to put a good face on things. Sounds great, I thought. Just what I need.

Eventually, of course, it was my turn to have everyone over. I made all the necessary preparations and looked forward to a rewarding time of devotion and reflection.

Ten minutes before guests arrived, however, I learned that two additional families would be joining us. No problem, I thought, we can stretch the food. I couldn't feed 5,000 with loaves and fishes, but waffles for about twenty shouldn't be a problem. I was happy get to know more people.

"Load up your plates," I announced after Ty said grace. "There should be plenty of seating outside at the picnic tables."

What followed caught me by surprise. I hadn't planned on all of our friends, along with their hungry kids, piling up in the Whetstone living room, paper plates full of food, picking their way through confused ranch boys and even more confused evening staff, in a futile attempt to find our backyard. I should have remembered there is no exit to the outside from "our side" of the house. I had mistakenly assumed they could figure out how to get there.

Since we were busy doling out food to go all the way around, our guests didn't know who to ask for help. Awkward stares lined the room, as if they were all from another country and didn't know how to speak the language.

Do we say hi? Ask for directions? Talk about the weather?

One guest, who actually found her way outside, was unceremoniously attacked by a bat that found its way into her hair.

A bat. In her hair!

Her arms flailing until the creature disentangled itself, she provided quite the spectacle through the window that most guests were staring through and wishing it were a door.

It was horrible about the bat, but I couldn't help thinking about the waffle that went flying off her plate! We needed it.

Eventually, after navigating around the boys who were eating a separate dinner, and gathering the courage to move in the direction of dive-bombing bats, the rest of the group settled outside. Conversation started to spring up—talk of kids, and jobs.

A few small bumps in the road so far, I thought, but we could laugh nervously about the food shortage and the flying rodent. Until...

"Ahhhh!" Someone screamed. "A snake!"

It was, as fate would have it, the daughter of the bat lady. She had stumbled upon a six-foot black snake—harmless enough, but not the kind of thing you want to see on the ground after your mom has been attacked from the skies.

Meanwhile, I had carefully calculated that if I skipped out on food entirely, if Ty ate only half a waffle, and if my three young boys consumed the other half, we just might have enough for everyone else.

I would just sit and sip my coffee. Maybe no one would notice.

Legs crossed, eyes to the ground, I glanced left to discover the mom seated next to me raising a last bite of syrupy waffle to her mouth . . . with her fingers.

I was confused.

"Hey," I inquired. "Would you like a fork?"

"No, it's okay," she answered, smiling. "I'm done now."

I soon discovered that she wasn't the only one eating her waffle without a fork.

"No forks?" I thought, starting to think I was stuck in some nightmare where everything comes up short.

I could have easily retrieved more forks from the Whetstone side, but it had slipped my mind. I hadn't accounted for the extra guests. And more horrifying, no one had said anything, sticky fingers and all.

Like all good hosts, I want my guests to feel at home.

At home, you dig through the kitchen drawers when you need something. Sure, you may find a few other things along the way like rubber bands and old packs of Life Savers, but you look anyways.

Especially if you're eating syrupy waffles.

Chapter 30

Spot

Matt

We are all drawn to dogs because they are the uninhibited creatures we wish we could be if we weren't certain we knew better.
—George Bird Evans

I've worked with some ridiculously talented therapists—world-renowned leaders in their fields of trauma, addiction, attachment. You name it. I've sat at their feet and worked alongside them. I've soaked in their wisdom and cut my therapeutic teeth under their tutelage. I'm confident in my abilities because of their mentoring.

And not a one of us could hold a candle to a good therapy dog.

Over the years, I've worked with several hundred pure-bred, AKC-registered Labradors in a therapeutic environment. They are miracle workers. It is not an overstatement to say I have witnessed them save lives.

But in all this time, I've never seen a dog as therapeutic as a blue heeler mutt that just showed up at the ranch one day. No papers, no training, no qualifications. It was like she had been born to do this.

Before I had a chance to weigh in on the matter, the boys named her Spot—after the big black spot on her rump. At first, it hurt my creative heart because I just love to name things. But the more I thought about, the more I liked it.

We live in an isolated spot. Our boys are in "a tight spot." The Bible relates stories about spotted calves, spotted sheep, spotted garments, spotted people.

She's weathered many storms at Whetstone, Spot. She's been loved and despised, bearing the brunt of great frustrations and misplaced affection. She's herded our adolescent crew with her little momma heart, checking on every boy who wanders this property. Every time someone makes a run for it, which happens on occasion, she has followed after, dodging rocks and sticks and frisbees flung at her in a desperate attempt to get her to leave them alone. But she never does.

She followed one guy ten miles to town. He felt so bad that he brought her home in the back of a state trooper's cruiser.

I have watched amazed as Spot has conducted expert sessions of grief counseling.

I witnessed her magic once with a boy who had just lost his mother. This occurred in the weeks following our reopening after the tornado, and I wasn't exactly in the best shape to provide the help he needed. To be honest, I needed the same help myself.

Enter Spot.

She sidled up to him, raised her paw to rest on his thigh, and waited. Waited for him to call her in.

Sitting cross-legged on the ground, in confused and stymied tears, the boy invited that dirty, dusty, tick-infested dog into his lap. She nuzzled her muzzle right between his shoulder and head, and he leaned on her and wept.

Eventually the young man gathered himself. The tears stopped. Spot trundled off.

But then, not long after, she invited herself back. She resumed her position, and he continued weeping.

I sat beside them the entire time, amazed, and unaware of time.

You don't count time in holy moments.

Chapter 31

FALSE HOPE

Axel

It's Wednesday, and since the boys are usually off-campus on a community service project in the middle of the week, I'm alone in my subterranean office, listening to *Kind of Blue*, drinking strong coffee, and working on the ranch's website. It's something I've been in charge of since we opened four years ago. I've also been the social media guy, spreading the word on Facebook, Twitter, and Instagram. I try to funnel all the traffic through whetstoneboysranch.com and raise the Google rankings. It's all about the analytics, baby.

Today I'm touting the low staff-to-boy ratio. The scenic Ozark setting. The experience of our staff. Our focus on relationship and mentoring and family. I'm highlighting our wonderful house parents, our work program, and our rigorous academics.

All of this coincides with the launch of a cutting-edge, mobile-friendly site that takes advantage of all the new bells and whistles. The last time we thought about web design, Barack Obama was still a junior senator from Illinois. The rest of the house is getting a facelift; why not the website?

But today it doesn't feel quite right.

Maybe it's because this afternoon one of our boys crawled out of his bedroom window in broad daylight, traipsed across the roof, shimmied down a ladder, and escaped without a trace into the Missouri wilderness.

We tried to find him for about thirty minutes even though we sensed the hopelessness of our search. This is the young man's second attempt. If a boy wants to run from us, we're not equipped to give chase. Neither are we equipped to really stop him in the first place. Could we have prevented this escape? Maybe. Could we stop him tomorrow, and the next day, and the day after that? No.

Runners gonna run.

We alert the proper authorities and wait for the blue flashing lights to bring him back. That's assuming the ticks don't get to him first.

All of this has got me feeling downright sad. Who runs away from a "wonderland of creativity and joy," as Whetstone was described in some of our original materials. Who sets out on a blistering hot day, with a heat index in the triple digits, without water and before dinner? Who does that?

I know I shouldn't take these things personally, and I don't . . . really. Not very much that is.

But when you're working on a website that will be seen at two o'clock in the morning by hundreds of desperate parents who can't sleep for distress over their lost boy, who are watching all their earthly dreams fall apart in the second semester of their son's freshman year, you don't want to give them false hope. Not after everything they've been through.

They might not survive another disappointment.

I know all of this sounds terribly depressing and quite possibly more than you bargained for. Like you picked up an inspirational tale about a boys ranch and somehow stumbled into Kurtz, Marlow, and *Heart of Darkness*.

I'm certain that there is light at the end of the tunnel. I just can't see it right now. Right now, I'm depressed about having to build a boys ranch from what feels like scratch for the second time in four years. I'm running pretty low on hope.

Maybe it's not the best day to work on the website.

Chapter 32

FORKS, PT. 2

Michelle

The morning after the waffle incident, my muscles ached like I had run a half marathon without any training. I moved through the motions, but my heart was sore. I decided to be helpful and heat up the leftovers for lunch so the other staff, specifically Axel, didn't have to do that when lunchtime came around. My boys Landon and Kellen sat at the island in the ranch kitchen. We were having a good moment. I listened attentively as they talked and ate. That's all I noticed.

I didn't notice the tapping of their stool legs.

The kitchen, you see, sits on top of the schoolroom beneath. Any repetitive sound is amplified by the silence of Axel's carefully monitored learning environment. Unbeknownst to me, he was busy fielding complaints from the boys about "that tapping sound."

I heard Axel come up the stairs, two steps at a time. He's a fast walker. I've noticed that about him. Maybe it's leftover from his West Point days.

Out he popped from the basement door and strode straight up to Kellen. Without addressing me, he asked my son to stop rocking the bar stool back and forth. The quiet tapping was really loud downstairs. Simple, direct, and not exactly out of line, but it bothered me.

I wanted to say something, but in my heart of hearts, I did not want to be disrespectful to him in front of my kids. I bit down hard on my tongue.

I knew I needed to talk to Axel, and if he had any sense of the momma bear lurking at the stove, he probably knew he needed to talk to me.

Overreacting is so easy to do when you live at Whetstone. Things easily become personal.

Later on, in a private conversation with him, I learned that a particular resident had spearheaded the complaints about my son's rocking while he was trying to do schoolwork.

"I don't care what M— thinks," I told Axel. "One minute he's best friends with my boys, the next minute he flat out ignores them. Talk about confusing. I don't care what he thinks. I care about my kids who have to live in this confusing environment. And I don't want any more rules for my kids on that side of the house. I can't ask them to follow one more silly rule."

The next day after my direct and straightforward conversation with Axel, I felt sad and disappointed. He wasn't being "silly." He wasn't trying to go around my authority as a mom to correct my kid and make a huge point. He just had a frustrated boy downstairs whom he was trying to help.

And how could he have known I was just a few hours removed from the humiliation of a disastrous small group Bible study—about the bat, and the strange boundaries of this living space, and the snake, and the recurring doubts about my role as a mom to both my children and other moms' children?

How could he have known about the forks?

Chapter 33

SYLVIA PLATH

Matt

"Filling a bucket." That's how Axel and I refer to school mornings at Whetstone. We make sure the boys can conjugate verbs, solve for the variable, and stay within the lines. It is accomplished because some things just need accomplishing.

But the afternoon, that's a whole different ball game. If the morning is "filling a bucket," then the afternoon is "lighting a fire." We dissect movies as we contemplate themes and motifs. We dive into the sound and sense of poetry. We sample the trove of vinyl records stored in Axel's office. We listen to their rich sounds, examine the album art, and then discuss the social and historical significance of artists like Beethoven, the Beatles, and Blondie. We explore the resonance of their ideas. We fill up a gratitude journal, write stories, discover inner heroes, and conquer hidden demons. It's active, group-centered, and a lot more exciting than mandatory schoolwork.

If Axel were reading this right now, he would be quick to lecture that from a transcript standpoint the afternoon is just as important as the morning. He'd go on and on about the marked difference between core subjects and electives, but that both are required for graduation. He'd also make certain you understood afternoons involve some easily overlooked instruction in the art of note taking, writing, speaking, listening, study skills, test taking, group dynamics, and a host of other skills necessary for success in college and in the workplace. Long story short, Axel would lovingly inform you that both morning and afternoon syllabi are integral to a well-rounded, liberal arts education.

It's on these afternoons that I love working with Axel. He's a good planner. It's one of his many gifts. He can lecture on a musical artist the boys have never heard of and connect that artist's work with his or her influence on whatever garden-variety pop music the rest of us simpletons listen to in our ignorance.

I wasn't keenly aware of the word *subgenre* before coming to Whetstone. Now I can name theatrical subgenres like sword-and-sandal, camp, film noir, and biopic as well as make a meaningful distinction between the 7,000 rock subgenres: prog rock, art rock, punk rock, jazz rock, mechanical rock, glam rock, space rock, nerd rock, and arena rock. Don't even get me started on post-rock.

Not too long ago, before the tornado, Axel had the boys read a poem by Sylvia Plath. He had given it to me earlier in the day to look over since we were trying something new that afternoon. I read it twice, understanding it less and less, until I remembered Axel's "First Rule of Understanding Poetry." *Always look at the title.* He's right. It makes a difference—even though the first time he went over that point with me, I thought it was a little obvious. "Who doesn't read a title before reading a poem?"

Ummm . . . me?

Directly above the first line in the Plath poem, clear as day, was the simple word "Mirror." Even though the one-word title is never mentioned again throughout the entirety of the poem (its absence being a very important sub-point in the Axel Liimatta School of Poetry: Rule 1 on Titles), it brought context and meaning to what I might have described three minutes previously as blabbering gibberish from an obviously disturbed person. (It also didn't help that Axel told me of her untimely demise before I read the poem, but I digress). The awareness of the title provided me with a better sense of the piece, and I didn't cast it aside as another poem in the long line of things I don't get right away and am therefore done with.

That afternoon when we read it with the boys, they followed Rule 1 and got the gist of the poem far more quickly than I did. Axel walked them through it, one step at a time, since we do this every Thursday afternoon. Then we read the poem aloud again because, according to Axel, you just don't "get" a great poem in the first couple tries. Only after this were we ready to talk about what we "got" out of it.

Thus, a two-hour conversation commenced, led predominantly by some very insightful teenage boys about voices of truth, identity, and accurate self-awareness—none of which are directly addressed within the poem about a lady who stares in a mirror and sees a fish.

There are some things you just can't plan. We didn't plan the tornado. But we are up and running again. We have boys in the beds and at the desks. We may be short a couple buildings and a bunch of trees, but we gained some pretty important things along the way. It gave Axel and me the opportunity to restructure our afternoon sessions: to sharpen minds and shape hearts. We are now better positioned to capitalize on unplanned opportunities that will continue to come.

On that afternoon with Sylvia Plath, poetry turned into a swelling discourse, and we had to cancel the two-mile run. It wasn't because the boys were avoiding it or because the staff didn't feel like it.

We weren't running away from life; we were running towards it.

Chapter 34

THE DARK KNIGHT

Axel

Some people see superheroes as superfluous. To these sort, the Marvel and DC universes are giant time sucks for losers who can't make it in the real world. Stan Lee embodies all that is wrong with a society that prefers to live out its dreams in CGI.

These naysayers may concede that Superman and Batman are fine to adorn the pajamas of an eight-year-old, but genuine adults outgrow these particular delusions of grandeur when they reach an appropriate age. The cutoff varies arbitrarily, but a forty-year-old for sure should not enjoy dressing up in stretchy pants . . . or enjoy watching others dress up in stretchy pants.

Real adults should not indulge voyeuristic fantasies by spending hard-earned dollars on a comic book or the outrageous ticket price to see the latest box office release of *Iron Man* or *Thor*. Legitimate messes exist in the world—like the one left by the tornado—that need real people who can face it squarely. You can't wish away a fallen tree. "Wingardium Leviosa" works all good and well at Hogwarts but not in Mountain View, Missouri.

Real cleanup crews wear Carhartts and Wranglers. And they don't wear masks.

Others see a problem with the entire fabric of the Marvel universe which, to them, seems couched in male chauvinism and racial stereotype. The women are generally in *need* of a hero. And even the heroines present body-image problems for any naïve young girl aspiring to walk in their ridiculous stilettos. (*You can't seriously fight crime when it takes all your effort to avoid slipping on the pavement.*)

Minorities, if they have the misfortune of being allied with the good guys, are the first to die. (Black Panther would be the exception that proves the rule.) And recasting traditionally white superheroes with black actors meets with such a backlash from the fan base, that studios quake at even the hint of a rumor that this might happen to an adaptation of their beloved hero. A black Superman should not be an issue fifty years after the Civil Rights Movement.

Marginalized groups of every sort (from homeschoolers to homeboys) are lining up to complain that they are not represented on the big screen's biggest of sets.

Whetstone doesn't line up squarely on one side or the other. In fact, an informal poll will most likely reveal sharp divisions, so I don't claim to represent our official stance . . . although I do imagine myself capable of providing a little unbiased perspective at times . . . which is just another way of saying I think I'm almost always right.

Don't we all?

Even people who say they are wrong most of the time, claim to be right about the fact that they are indeed wrong. And even if they were wrong about this, they would still be right—in being wrong about their wrongness. We just can't get around the idea that right exists. We don't always know what it is, for sure, but we *can* be sure that it's out there.

And this explains why I think superheroes are important. They exist because they need to exist. You can call them whatever you want: Moses or Macbeth, Sisyphus or Superman, John Wayne or Bruce Wayne. They're an archetype that can only be avoided by repressing our true nature, which only results in a more powerful manifestation in the subconscious mind.

And if that is your situation, I wish you well. Good night and good luck.

For the rest of us, superheroes represent our recognizable and common desire to rise above and reach beyond. They represent everything we are, can be, are not, and hope to become. So at Whetstone, we don't try to rob boys of their childish imaginings.

Let's use the Dark Knight as an example. Not Batman, but the Dark Knight. Big difference.

Over the weekend, the boys watched the first two films in Christopher Nolan's trilogy, starring Christian Bale as the caped crusader. Along with many other assignments that allow boys to earn a "Film Studies" credit on their school transcript, they are required to ponder why Bruce Wayne *chooses* to become the Dark Knight.

Why does he take the blame for Harvey Dent's death? Why does he agree to be the villain? Why does he let himself be chased, hunted, and scapegoated? Beyond that, why does he wear the mask to begin with? What is he hiding? Exactly when does he become the Dark Knight? Will the real Dark Knight please stand up? Please stand up?

Their answers were penetrating, often revealing more about themselves than about the film. No one else would accept responsibility. False guilt. His father's legacy. A misguided sense of justice . . .

Suddenly, I was in a college-prep English class. This was a deep and meaningful conversation, not only because the boys were engaging their minds, but because their life experiences prepared them for heavier burdens.

Matt and I often find this to be the case. Our boys understand many things your run-of-the-mill teenager doesn't.

That's a bad thing on many occasions, unfortunately.

But on the days when we probe the shadowy recesses of the Dark Knight and examine the psychological implications of his martyr complex, it's a good thing.

It's a really good thing.

Chapter 35

PIGS

Michelle

There are usually several guys on the Whetstone staff who aren't boys but who aren't very far removed from boyhood themselves.

These young adults have not grown old, and they have not stopped dreaming. They have wild ambitions, wonderful amounts of energy, and a deep love for our boys. Their story is often similar to the boys placed in our care, and they can relate to them on a level that a house mom never could. They carry a common burden.

They are the "mentoring specialists."

That's what we call them here at the ranch. That was Joey's position and title when the tornado struck. Our mentoring specialists have the maturity and experience to know they can't ride out a storm by pretending it doesn't exist, while being adventurous enough to own survival gear that actually gets put to use on the weekend.

It's the mentoring specialist who picks up the slack when my husband is not around to help unload the groceries or open the canned peaches. To explain this, let's travel back in time…

I'm seven months pregnant, and the ranch pigs have somehow escaped from the pen. They move greedily and ever so close to our freshly planted garden. My son Landon is five years old and his brother Kellen is four. We are the only ones at Whetstone on this particular afternoon. Ty is working, which on this occasion means he's playing golf with the boys off campus. They are too far away to help.

And I need help. I can't get these pigs put up by myself. Pigs can be mean, gnarly creatures. Not at all like Wilbur in *Charlotte's Web*. "Please and thank you" just aren't in these critters' vocabulary.

After thirty minutes of unsuccessful pig wrangling, a black SUV pulls up onto the property. Two guys in white shirts and dark ties hop out.

"Ah, I've had to do that before," one of the neatly dressed men mentions as he walks up to me and then, without missing a beat, launches into his testimony.

We're going to do this right now?

Thankfully, miraculously, our mentoring specialist at the time peels into the drive. It's Troy to the rescue.

Troy tells the visitors kindly but firmly that we don't have time for long talks about salvation. We have to get these pigs put up. The shirts and ties nod in agreement then turn to leave.

Tracts in hand, Troy and I walk back towards where the hogs have migrated. The SUV speeds away down the dirt road.

Later, I think about these two guys. They weren't bad people. But they certainly weren't what I needed at the time. I needed someone who could help get the pigs in their pen.

At Whetstone, we do our fair share of witnessing. We walk and talk. We teach and preach. Direct instruction has its place.

But the best work we do is when we quietly sit with a boy who is homesick. It's when we listen, really listen to a boy who feels he isn't being heard, who might even feel that he hasn't been heard, even once, in his entire life.

Our very best work is when we help him to get a handle on the conflicting emotions of adolescence that sometimes run free like pigs on a prison break.

Chapter 36

Dictionary

Matt

My wife, Jessica, tells me that my words are too big. When she does, I apologize and inform her that I have no intention of being sesquipedalian. She will roll her eyes and say, "You mean loquacious." On a good day, I might counter with, "More like verbose," but her retort typically forces me to accept defeat and consult a dictionary. You'd think I know by now that it's a game I can't really win. She has a stranglehold on the English language. As in most encounters with my wife, I am outwitted before the game ever starts.

She's right, though. I do tend to use words that can be a bit out of reach for the average twelve to fifteen-year-old. But you know what? I'm perfectly fine with that.

A wise man once told me that words create worlds. There was a being, and there was a void, and then silence was broken with words. It was the first invitation, the greatest, "Let there be light!" I remember reading in Barbara Brown Taylor's book, *When God Is Silent*, that up until the creation of Adam, God had a monopoly on speech. He brought forth cosmos from logos. Words have been creating worlds ever since. God creates human beings, makes them in His image, male and female, and lets them speak. They become creators.

Even the absence of words is formative. This same world that was spoken into existence was radically transformed through the silence of the One who spoke it so.

Abba, Father.

My God, my God?

His response? To his only begotten Son?

Silence.

Greater writers have written greater, more eloquent books on such things.

In grad school, one learns that many, many studies on human communication, both latitudinal and longitudinal, are filled with fancy conclusions; but the first and most important is that one cannot *not* communicate. I loved it. Not only because it was a double negative, which I won't say I don't love, but because it rang true.

At Whetstone we live in a world of constant interruption. We house a bunch of boys gifted in, and incredibly frustrated by, interruption. You should be a fly on the wall during dinner some evening. (*Consider this your invitation.*) Whether we're solving deep theological issues or deciphering whether or not illiterate people get the full effect of alphabet soup, opinions are so readily tossed back and forth that the dining room table is transformed into a proverbial spittoon. One voice rises above the next, each competing for attention, each screaming in its own way, to be heard. Even a boys' silence during such times can be deafening.

Occasionally one opinion flies in from left field, somewhere so far removed from the present conversation that everything halts, as if some stranger just wandered through the swinging saloon doors. It is followed by a hushed silence, raised eyebrows, bated breath, and then finally, a rush of derision and laughter. The uninvited are not welcome here.

On other occasions, that left-field comment brings a hush of sober resonance. The speaker has brought a perspective previously unconsidered but desperately needed. Everyone nods in quiet agreement, or maybe someone pantomimes having their "mind blown."

Which is why the boys bring a dictionary into their hour-long counseling sessions each week: *Webster's New Collegiate*

Dictionary, the one with a red cloth cover.

Like many good things, what was born out of necessity has become a meaningful tradition. Sometimes they forget, and if you're in the school room, you might see a guy run back to his desk, grab his dictionary, and scramble back to my office in a red-tinted blur. This means we have stumbled upon a word that he, or I, don't really know. Or perhaps we suspect that the word doesn't exactly mean what we think it means. *Inconceivable*!

The boy needs to know words, not have them dumbed down to textspeak or lower-grade levels. He needs to know some of the jargon of therapy. He needs to know how to express himself. He needs to know that his comment isn't just mean; it is *caustic*. He needs to know that he's not just upset; he's *indignant*. He needs to know that his parents aren't just worrying about him; they are *agonizing* about his absence from their dinner table each night.

He needs to be handed keys to unlock doors to new worlds. And if the words aren't there, then he needs to be granted the power to create them!

Because words, when all is said and done, are all we have to go on. We deconstruct them to our own demise. For Moses spoke to the rock in the desert, and Jesus spoke to Lazarus' grave. "Come forth!"

Without words, we lose the power to create, the power to build, and (more important to Whetstone) we lose the power to *re*-build: a family, a home, a house, a ranch.

Words reframe a sad and tragic story.

They change the narrative from defeat to victory—from deep and abiding loss, to long and abounding joy.

Chapter 37

REFRAME

Axel

We all do it. Some of us are better at it than others. Boys placed at Whetstone are truly masters of the craft.

It's a double-edged sword.

Someone calls you a fool, a clown, or a goofball.

At first you recoil, knowing that deep down God created you for higher things. For poetry and music. For truth and beauty. For infinity and beyond, not this vaudevillian joke of an existence. Not Prometheus chained to a juvenile pejorative.

You retreat into yourself for a few hours, or days, or weeks. You ask yourself, "Is this really who I am? Am I really what other people think of me? Do I not get some say in the matter?"

And then in your deepest moment of existential angst, you discover a way out.

You decide to *be* what other people think you *are*. Problem solved!

What appeared to be a dead end becomes a way of escape. You have subverted the system, turned it upside down and inside out. Like Superman in the crystal cave, you reconfigure the chamber to expose the villains while protecting yourself.

Gotcha!

Our mortal enemies will now crumple before us. Their strength has vanished.

For days, weeks, sometimes years afterwards, we feel liberated.

We relish the role of getting sent to the principal's office. We look forward to the reactions we arouse in others: shaking heads, wagging fingers, pursed lips. We move people like puppets. With the slightest flick of our wrist or tilt of our arm, we make them dance the farandole.

We parade around, all sound and fury. The entirety of our life is a stage.

And then one day the darkness descends like a heavy curtain. The moment comes when we realize we have been playing the fool to everyone's delight but our own. Infamous does not mean "more than famous." We have defined our terms all wrong. What now? Now that we are chained in our cave, backs to the light, watching the shadowy puppet shows of our lives.

Now, we will be loyal to the nightmare of our choice.

But what if we could go back?

What if we could reframe the reframe? What if we could see ourselves as God saw us then and sees us now? Confused. Battered. Bewildered. Struggling for an identity that does not exist outside of ourselves. Outside of that which He created us to be.

What if we could go back to that kid who questioned himself and talk to him?

We can, you know. We do this kind of time travel all the time.

We feel self-pity. We armchair ourselves to death and silently scream at such levels that real communication becomes virtually impossible, the interior monologue of our stream of consciousness drowning out all reason.

Our boys represent an extreme case. Abandoned. Abused. Neglected. They tell themselves over and over as one boy confessed to me: "I'm a piece of sh**. I'm a piece of sh**. I'm a piece of sh**." It had become his mantra, a twisted kind of centering-prayer.

Stuck on replay and without anyone to tell him otherwise, how can he make sense of all the garbage heaped down upon his head and not become buried alive beneath a rotting pile of refuse?

Easy. He becomes synonymous with it. That's the path of least resistance. *Hello darkness, my old friend.* His dark hole becomes his only comfort in all its stinking paradox.

But here's the thing. The glorious, impossible thing!

Someone so adept at beating himself up about a past he has no control over, must also be capable of reimagining it. Such a person, it stands to reason, must intuitively embrace the notion that life is not what it seems but what he makes of it. Such a person understands the power of a story and of being part of a larger narrative—dare we say, even, a hero's journey.

And it is just such a person to whom God has spoken, time and time again. Abram reframed as Abraham. Jacob, Israel. Cephas, Peter. Saul, Paul.

Never again will you be called "The Forsaken City" or "The Desolate Land." Your new name will be "The City of God's Delight" for the Lord delights in you.

God is speaking to our boys.

You are not a prostitute, a leper, or a lunatic living among the tombs. You are a precious child of God.

A lost and wild thing maybe. Yes, truly. But a thing that God loves more than anything else.

And thus, if you listen, God speaks you into existence, reframing the entire nature of what is real and what will stand for all time as the essential, indivisible, and indissoluble you.

Chapter 38

SPENT

Michelle

"Mrs. Lew... Lew... Lewis? I... I... I don't think (*sniffle*)... I don't think I can do this. I just miss (*quick breath*) my family (*sniffle*) so much."

He leans in for a hug.

He's been here two days.

I feel terribly sorry, but I'm just not comfortable letting him cry on my shoulder or letting him give me a big hug. I will give him many hugs over the next few months, but for now as Matt tells me, my response is part of setting healthy boundaries.

That doesn't make it feel any less awkward.

I have him sit down, pull up a chair beside him, and pat him on the arm.

"You're going to be okay," I say. "You're going to make it. Just get through today. That's all you have to worry about right now. I know for a fact that every boy who has ever come here has been scared and sad. Even the ones who pretend they aren't."

We sit together in silence.

"You're not alone," I say.

I want to cry, to show him I care. But the one time I want some tears to come, they leave me hanging.

Good one, Michelle. You really saved the day.

Sometimes, I wonder why God has me here to work with

teenage boys.

Having grown up with a sister, I feel like I know the girl thing pretty well. Dolls, dress up, dancing and, of course, girls' team sports.

But boys? During family get-togethers in my childhood, one set of boy cousins chased me and pulled my hair out. Another boy cousin told me scary tales of copperhead snakes and bobcats.

Boys? They lie, and they're mean. Even the cute ones . . . especially the cute ones.

Of course, I married a boy, but not a teenage one, and thankfully not one that lies to me.

And he hasn't pulled my hair out yet.

Still, I feel like I need a how-to manual on most days.

Sometimes I feel very uncomfortable being the only woman at Whetstone. So much so that when a boy asks to talk, I feel the need to double-check with Ty. Maybe he knows what it's about and how I should handle it. Because I honestly have little insight into what's really going on in their lives. I'm not involved with counseling. I don't read their files. From what I can gather, their files don't tell you much anyway. It's the stuff we don't know about them that causes most of the problems. As Matt says, you don't know what you don't know.

I go to staff meetings when I can, but often I have to stay with my own boys.

I guess when a boy at Whetstone needs to talk, I should pray first. I don't want to say something stupid or simply share my own bit of made-up wisdom.

I want it to be what God needs the young man to hear, know, and believe. Otherwise, what's the point?

God wants to heal. He *longs* to be gracious towards us.

This should make us gracious towards others, willing to share and to listen. It should motivate us to take time out of our busy schedules, always paying attention to divine appointments.

Before long, the theory goes, we might actually desire to do so.

Such pondering thoughts inspired me to write the following poem.

Frozen

Time
stands still
in a freezer.

Beef and broth
see no decay,
and the fresh
breath of life –

red, yellow, green
seed, fruit, or bean –

keeps
needs to come,
and plans to be:

bags and bags
of food
dumped down,
thrown in,
covered, and buried
by frost.

This cold manna
stings my fingers
to the bone.

Beneath
heavy blocks
of meat,

I find
breast milk
for a baby
I no longer feed—

filled with life
that once emptied me.

I won't say much about the poem because Axel tells me a good poem doesn't need my help. I *will* say it's about cleaning the freezer while we waited for the boys to return after the tornado. Beyond that, I will only say that it is about the difficulties of feeding a family.

I feel responsible for my husband, myself, my three boys, and an ever-changing number of teenage boys with teenage stomachs. It's draining.

However, at the end of the day, when the house mom gets to bask in a dozen contented smiles floating above an equal number of empty plates at the dinner table, she feels like it has all been worth the effort.

She knows that W—, who arrived at the ranch with his ribs showing like a washboard, has gained twenty pounds because of her.

She knows that B—, a boy who survived on potato chips and chicken fingers for far too long, has color in his cheeks because of her.

She knows that R—, who hadn't eaten a vegetable since second grade, will add years to his life and life to his years because he no longer pretends to gag every time his tongue touches a tomato.

When she puts her head down on her pillow at night, she rests well—drained, but content that the time with all her boys has been well spent.

Chapter 39

CASABLANCA

Matt

Rick Blaine isn't the best representation of an emotionally balanced individual. (*Name for me a hero who is.*) In fact, when we first meet Rick in the film *Casablanca*, he's probably at his worst. He's calculatingly cold in his indifference, with no respect for man, woman, or beast. He has distanced and detached himself from other people so effectively that he is synonymous with the neon light that hangs in the darkness above the entrance to his self-proclaimed gin joint. He *is* Rick's. It takes a lot of effort to look that effortless.

If you haven't seen *Casablanca*, you're missing out on a hearty slice of cinematic pie. It's a timeless classic that continues to resonate with audiences more than seventy years after its release. How do I know? Because I just had a two-hour discussion about a black-and-white film with six teenage boys who found a little piece of their story, if not their soul, wrapped up tightly within the movie's one hour and forty-two minutes.

The year is 1942. People flee from German-occupied Europe in hopes of making it to America by acquiring the necessary and all important "letters of transit." Some make it out by their own fortune, influence, or even luck, but the vast majority of desperate souls "wait in Casablanca . . . and wait, and wait, and wait."

It is here that we find Rick running his eponymous café,

profiting from all the people caught in limbo as they dream of freedom while he supports them with his "healing waters." Rick can't go back, and he can't leave. He's made his place here. Like it or not, it's as home as anywhere's gonna be after everything he's been through.

A good number of the film's nuances escape the boys. They don't truly understand the tension between the French Resistance and the German occupation of northern Africa. During rousing scenes of patriotism that move the participants to tears, the boys don't fully grasp the weight of a world at war. It's a confusing scene for them until I explain it. Even then, they may claim to understand just so they won't have to talk about it anymore.

But when you bring up Rick, every face around that table lights up with an understanding glow. They know a tumultuous, downtrodden existence because they've been there. They're on the same journey he is, moving towards vulnerable without being weak.

You see, it's a couple days before one boy's first family intensive, and another's will follow shortly thereafter. A family intensive is a heavy-duty therapy session that explores family patterns and exposes demons of all those involved. To say these two young men are nervous is a gross understatement. It's taking everything in their beings to not explode on everyone around them. They're triggered by every little movement. Eyes dart back and forth, looking for a reason to blow.

I wouldn't call these boys ticking time bombs because "ticking" implies some warning will precede the explosion. These boys have dropped the "ticking" and the "time." They are all bomb!

There's no way around it. Many of our boys struggle with post-traumatic stress, and this place feels like a hurt locker at times; we just happen to be the safest place to detonate.

The boys' parents will come to town, and they'll sit with me for hours of intense family therapy. We'll dig into their life stories, the patterns passed down through generations, and the languages of relationship.

They're scared. Not of their parents, not necessarily of their stories . . . well, maybe just a little. Mostly, they're just afraid of the unknown. The awkwardness of relating to their parents in a different way. They are afraid of understanding and of connecting. And they are deathly afraid of discovering that their worst fear is really true: that they're either not worth the effort or so screwed up they're beyond hope.

Which is precisely why we watch *Casablanca*—because Rick has walked in their shoes. He's hurt, and he's been burnt, but he's found a way to deal with it. He may not be as bold or heroic as he was before, but it beats the alternative. There's something to be said for surviving. He famously "sticks his neck out for no one."

But slowly, as the movie progresses through all seven of the American Film Institute's Top 100 Movies Quotes, you see and hear him return to the man he was.

To be sure, he has moments when he regresses, moments where you wish he wasn't such a jerk, but he also has those shining moments when you see him, the real him.

In memorable Parisian flashbacks, we witness his pain and grief as he reads the rain-soaked note that tells him Ilsa has left him for Victor Laszlo. This wrenching heartbreak puts Rick's life choices in perspective for us, and the story now looks very different. The questions start to flow as freely as the libations Rick pours each night.

How do you deal with pain? How do you deal with pain caused by someone you love? How do you deal with pain caused by someone you love when it isn't his or her fault? How do you let others deal with their pain while you struggle to deal with yours?

It's a family intensive wrapped inside a movie, mirroring the process of how our boys must begin to put their story in context with their family history. It doesn't stop the pain, but it does alter how they deal with it, and that's what we're after. It might be true that "the problems of three little people don't amount to a hill of beans in this crazy world," but that doesn't mean we can't use those beans to plant something bigger.

We change the frame as we move forward.

Family intensives consist of two parts. The first part frames everything as part of a story. *Rounding up the usual suspects*, so to speak. I work with the parents and their son to find patterns of thought and behavior as well as underlying causes. I heard once that if you don't understand someone's behavior, it's only because you don't understand their story. Even the most illogical responses can be explained with context. The family intensive is a pretty big undertaking for everyone involved, and it requires an uncomfortable level of vulnerability.

But if everyone plays their part, it works. There is reconciliation. They all start to see each other in a different light. They will come together.

I've lost count of the number of young men who have told me, "I can't believe they felt that way, too. I thought I was the only one."

For the adolescent mind and heart, this can be information overload. Guys need a little time to unpack it all, so we hug and part ways for a few weeks or, sometimes, months.

This waiting period provides excellent teachable moments. I help point out the difference between intimacy and intensity, and the lasting power of process. If family relationship is only built in moments of intensity, even intense therapy, then the pattern of cultivating intensity to seek connection will only perpetuate.

So we give the intensive session a little bit of time, process how it went, what we've learned, what it changes "as time goes by." Understanding his parents' story starts to shift the boy's reaction. He begins to see why his parents reacted so strongly to his behaviors.

During the second family intensive, both the parents and the boy must come to terms with how they've acted, what they've done and failed to do. They must express the resentment and the regret. Take ownership of ways in which they've hurt each other and start treating each other with respect.

"I can handle it," I tell the boy to tell himself.

"You are not *too much*," I tell the parents to tell their son.

The relationship won't break down if they break some of the old rules. Intensity does not equal intimacy. They don't need sparks and fire and alternating periods of the cold dark to be in relationship.

They need to kill some of the sacred cows that used to crap in their living room.

The second intensive also serves as a kind of Ebenezer. It's a marker on the family's journey, standing as testament that God showed up. I like to think we are Israelites crossing the Jordan into the Promised Land. We're sitting in my little office, stacking stones.

We'll always have Whetstone.

It's a powerful experience—when the previously unseen is finally seen for what feels like the first time.

In the awkwardness. In the tears and in the snot bubbles. (*Especially the snot bubbles.*) In the not knowing what to do next but still wanting to get back in the game.

In the moment when a mom and dad lift their baby boy's chin up to their tear-stained faces, look into his eyes, and say, "Here's looking at you, kid."

And if everyone wants it, I mean really *wants* it, we'll end our time with the reason we all ended up here in the first place: to look ahead and to dream about the future.

And we'll note in somber but hopeful tones that do not discount any of the undeniable pain in the past or inevitable struggle in the future:

"I think this is the beginning of a beautiful friendship."

Chapter 40

You Do You

Axel

Matt introduced me to this now ubiquitous phrase. It is one of many concise statements that have become part of my lexicon since he brought his borderline millennial worldview to Whetstone in 2013. And while it is true that many of his aphorisms are related to Chris Farley or Will Ferrell in some way, a great many have more clinical purposes.

This is not to say that a good El Niño impersonation is without therapeutic merit (*all other tropical storms bow before me* is indeed a good illustration of narcissism), but I was capable of providing those types of insights before we met.

"You do you" brings it to the next level.

When a boy seems intent on deflection, pointing everyone and everything away from personal responsibility. *You do you.*

When a young man complains that life is not fair, how someone else got an ounce or two more of Michelle's famous shepherd's pie. *You do you.*

When one of our guys is working through issues of abandonment, inadequacy, non-worth, and un-love. When he constantly and obsessively seeks attention because of a deep need for validation. *You do you.*

It just works. Backwards and forwards. *You do you.* Coming and going. It's a kind of sentence palindrome.

Jesus taught something similar when he encouraged his disciples not to worry about tomorrow. "Today has enough troubles of its own," he said.

You do you. Drop the scroll, rabbi.

When one apostle grew jealous of another—as in the case of Peter and John regarding the type of death they might suffer—Jesus literally said, "What is that to you? You must follow me."

There it is in red letters: *You do you*.

Still, months after the tornado, it's impossible to live without any worry or anxiety about the future. Jesus said some hard things—things that seem to go against my very nature.

You do you is a lot easier to say to others than to myself.

My worry is justified.

Whetstone still has bills to pay, and I am counting on that paycheck every two weeks. I'm having flashbacks to when we opened in 2011, and I'm not sure we can do it all over again. It took quite a few miracles to get us started the first time.

An evolutionary biologist might argue that our inclination to fret about the future is a natural byproduct of an advanced cognitive ability to plan for the future. Blame it on the prefrontal cortex, baby.

But nowadays, I'm guessing more people die from hypertension than failure to adequately prepare for the zombie apocalypse.

You do you.

Stop worrying about things you can't control.

You do you, Axel! Worrying won't add a single hair to your head, hour to your life, or cubit to your height.

You do you.

Chapter 41

#YouToo

Michelle

"I feel like a failure," the mother said as she navigated her way through the French toast and oozing syrup heaped up on her paper plate.

"You can't help but feel that as the parent, it's your fault," she continued. "I don't know what God's purpose was in His lack of protection of my children."

It was a sticky situation.

What could I tell her? I didn't know why He seems to protect sometimes and allow evil other times.

And this conundrum made her angry. It made me angry.

So we sat there, eating breakfast, while she anticipated the return of her son to her home after the two o'clock graduation that afternoon.

A son who was different but not fixed.

A son who would, without a doubt, continue to struggle.

She knew this. I knew this. We all know this every time we gather to celebrate a Whetstone graduation. To paraphrase C.S. Lewis, the joy now is part of the pain later.

On these occasions, we don't celebrate a beaming pinnacle of perfect success; we celebrate a boy and his willingness to persevere on some level.

He is, for all of his hard work, still a boy. A boy on his way to desired manhood but a boy nonetheless.

This perseverance looks different for everyone in our program.

For some, it looks like trying vegetables.

For others, it looks like allowing themselves to love.

For still others, it looks like letting someone cut their hair.

Or keeping their room clean, trying hard in school, running hard to beat a personal record, consistently showering and taking care of their teeth, smiling, being kind, apologizing... The list goes on and on.

Celebration can and should exist in the midst of struggle. You shouldn't wait until the process is complete or perfect. I am learning this lesson now, *because* of the tornado. There are moments of sticky, messy goodness that can only be celebrated as they happen—not before, and not after. After is too late.

On that day after filling our bellies with French toast and our hearts with the connection that comes from laughter, tears, and story, this boy's two Whetstone moms were ready to lift him up.

And at the very end of the ceremony, she courageously stood up in front of the gathered crowd, and tearfully took him into her arms. She looked him in the eyes and told him she loved him. Told him that he had experienced things no one on this earth should experience. She was honest about his faults; she was honest about what she expected. She was hopeful but not unrealistic.

I thought to myself, *"You go, mom!* You are a mother of a broken son whose brokenness is not your fault. You too have experienced things no one on this earth should experience. And you too continue to persevere."

And I wanted to say, "You are not a failure. No one at Whetstone thinks you have failed."

And I wanted to shout, "You are very much worth celebrating, too!"

Chapter 42

CAVES

Matt

Opposite our two new refrigerators and just before you leave the kitchen area, you run into a wall of black chalkboards filled with colorful writing. Pre-tornado, it was just a wall with a few cheap Walmart white boards. After the twister, I've grown fond of this new format, which is much more ornate. It's a morale booster. It says we care, I think.

The chalkboards boast nicely drawn calendars, filled with the month's appointments, events, and celebrations. This way an important trip to tighten a boy's braces doesn't get dropped, and a thirteenth birthday doesn't get overlooked. It is all done in good coffee house style with vibrant markers and even serif font at times. As the mood strikes, staff members will write a meaningful quote or two, just to add something else to catch the eye or heart.

At present someone has chalked up a Kierkegaard quote in precise cursive which pops out against the dark background.

"Love does not alter the beloved, it alters itself."

I could pretend that I know what this famous Danish existentialist meant when he wrote it, but even in context it befuddles me.

But it's not about me or the guys making sense of it. The quote is there, so we can have the conversation. And we do.

Often.

As I've said before, I'm surrounded by a house full of teenage philosophers.

The pioneering psychologist John Bowlby defines attachment as a "deep and enduring emotional bond that connects one person to another across time and space." Without getting into the depths of the issue here, it will suffice to say that attachment, or the lack thereof, plays an important role in relationships everywhere. How much more so at a boys ranch?

We tend to get a lot of guys struggling with what the mental health field refers to as "attachment issues." Even the most well-intentioned parents are not immune from sharing the fruit of multi-generational hurts and wounds with their kids. We live in a fallen, broken, hurting world, and it's going to impact all of us in one way or another.

I talked this morning with a mother from a family looking for help. Good parents, they adopted their son from birth and were well aware of their child's potential hurts and hang-ups. His problems weren't news to them, but the mother struggled to choose the right words to describe her son whose hurt was so deeply rooted that his behaviors mimicked that of someone half his age. "Despite all this," she said, "he's . . . well, he's an old soul."

I immediately knew what she meant. I've counseled some temper-tantrum-throwing infants who were old souls.

Roughly one third of the guys placed in our care have been adopted. I've worked with enough adoptees to let you know this. No matter how well it goes, having to be adopted is a deep, cutting wound that just doesn't go away on its own. We were created for attachment, and when it's taken away, the hurt is primal. How are you supposed to put words to a hurt that happened before you had words? You don't have to *learn* how to question who you are; you were born with an identity crisis. It's stuck, right there in the core of your very being, and that hurt brings nagging, unanswered questions, begging to be reckoned with—and despite your best efforts, refusing to be ignored. Do I look like my parents? Will I turn out to be like my parents?

Would my parents be proud of me?

At some point on my educational path, I had to read about Plato and philosophy and stuff like that. I did so somewhat reluctantly. I remember some story about a cave and Plato being upset because the Athenians killed his teacher Socrates for disrupting the social order. I don't remember why Plato wrote the story, just that it was about some prisoners who were trapped in a cave, and their only contact with the real world was through the shadows cast on the wall of the people who passed by outside. The prisoners understood nothing but shadows, facsimiles. Like the real thing but not the real thing. I remember being frustrated with the whole idea because I thought, "Well, why don't they just turn around?" But when my question wasn't immediately answered in class, I let it go.

I didn't have time for allegories; I had basketball practice.

One Sunday at Pomona Christian Church, Axel was scribbling furiously in a little writing journal he carries with him. I didn't think much of it because at some point every day, Axel's writing something in a journal.

It's none of my business, I thought to myself as I folded up my by-then-doodle-covered church bulletin out of guilt. A man could write whatever he wants in his journal at church. Maybe he doodled too—which would be ironic because in this case the man sat directly behind the Whetstone boys, some of whom dutifully took notes like he taught them. Meanwhile, my reasoning continued, he sat there and doodled. Classic. But what do I know? I'm just a doodler.

Come to find out Axel spent that time composing a poem:

Spark

    It's how I do us,
    this pushing, pulling
    kind of dance.

A tango tension
threatens to destroy—
and holds together
by its heat.

I am off-putting
from the start
not because I don't want to be with you,
but because being
(with you)
means looking like this.

I know no other way,
except the friction
and its fire.

Its heat and spark
mean something lives between—
reminding me I am not alone
and that the darkness where I dwell
is not
all
there is.

But when I see
the ugliness of you and me
lit by this flicker,
the monstrous shadows
shaped by light
drive me back into my cave

where all the voices
and all the visions
sing in veto to myself,

and we can be
no more.

He read it to me later, and it struck a chord. Those who have experience with attachment disorder can feel the heat from its push and pull, and the tension that it creates. With singed arm hair, you try to lead and then follow—in both cases moving dangerously close to the flame until the inevitable happens. You get burned.

No matter. Tomorrow we'll dance again as if nothing happened. Because intensity equals intimacy. This torturous tango is how we "do" relationship.

I hadn't thought of Plato in years, but while reading "Spark," I remembered the part where one prisoner gets free and encounters the outside world. He sees life for all it is, not just the shadows. He gets used to life outside the cave and starts to feel sorry for the other prisoners still chained inside. So he returns, desperate to explain how great life is outside the cave, that there is more to the world than the shadows. Much to his surprise, they want no part of it.

I don't remember entirely, but I'm pretty sure they aren't very nice when he tries to set them straight. (This must have been when the whole allegory thing grew tiresome for me.)

Anyway, there the free man sits, frustrated, too accustomed to the light to see the shadows but unable to convince the others.

I feel for Plato's character. How do you deal *with* shadows without being *in* them? When do you flee from a burning house, and when do you stay to fight the flames?

The boys devoured Axel's poem. We read "Spark" and had a two-hour conversation about it, each guy connecting parts of the poem with his world.

Like I said. Teenage philosophers.

Because attachment is an existential dilemma, in some ways these young men have a head start on the rest of us. They're always driving, pushing, searching, pulling, and hoping even if it's only in shadow.

Hopefully, they'll break the chains someday and learn a new dance.

I've been there too. I've retreated back to my cave, preferring the devil I know to the devil I don't. If we ever took time to look deep enough, we'd each have our own identity crisis. It's part of living in a fallen world.

Which is why the staff and our boys will sit and ponder a confusing Kierkegaard quote scrawled on a chalkboard. Not because we need to differentiate between existential and postmodern philosophy, but because we're trying to escape our caves of anxiety, apathy, fear, and indifference.

Chances are you have been a cave dweller yourself; you've been there too.

So if you're not too busy solving your own existential dilemma, pray that we'll all turn around and see the light.

Chapter 43

Tomorrow

Axel

His name is Shakespeare.
I don't know the full story. You rarely do when you work at a place where everyone else picks up where you left off and vice versa.

And that's okay. I don't need to know everything.

He's a cross between a mostly blue heeler and a stray dog of murky ancestry. (Remember Spot? She's the mom.)

Cute as can be. Wrinkly face. Droopy eyes. Good disposition. Some say mutts make the best dogs. Hybrid vitality at its best.

Michelle has given away all the other pups from Spot's litter. Shakespeare is the last. Parting is indeed such sweet sorrow.

Tomorrow, we're giving Shakespeare away as a graduation gift to M—. He's the only boy who returned after the tornado and finished the program. He sure seems like a changed young man. He's more self-aware and willing to accept that life is friction. He knows he will continue to have struggles with his parents. He won't be perfect. He might even relapse. He will almost certainly relapse.

But it will be okay. He can handle it. He is not too much for his parents to handle.

He can't eliminate all the doubt and fear and anger that his circumstances have brought to the surface. But they aren't hiding out anymore either. They are real emotions, and he needs to honor them—not push them away like some tragic hero.

Shakespeare should help.

Chapter 44

CHRISTMAS

Michelle

> *Take my yoke upon you, and learn from me,*
> *for I am gentle and lowly in heart,*
> *and you will find rest for your souls.*
> —Matthew 11:29

Christmas at a boys ranch is not easy.

For the boys, it is a visual reminder that their family is missing. All the little rituals which bring joy to most families are just as likely to pour wassail in their open wounds.

I get it. They are not "home for the holidays." But the mom in me wants to ask, "Can you try? Please? Just *try* to be happy?"

My first Christmas as a house mom, I was filled with holiday spirit. One might say I took things a little too far.

I expected the top of the tree to touch the ceiling and the lights to be so abundant that the living room would simply glow with the same holiday spirit I felt. Christmas music and hot chocolate would usher a new age of hope into the room.

Instead, the boys grumbled. They hated the music. Ty accidentally broke off the top of the carefully measured tree. And since one boy hung the lights all helter skelter, I took over and promptly poked myself in the eye with a jagged cedar branch.

The emergency room doctor informed me I was lucky; one more millimeter, and I would have been blind in that eye for the rest of my life. He prescribed Percocet and a week of bed rest.

Talk about not feeling holly or jolly.

The first Christmas after the tornado, I decided to lower my expectations.

The boys picked a beautiful tree. One boy worked crazy hard at straightening it, patiently twisting the metal bolts until it was close to perfect. Another wrapped strands upon strands of lights, starting at the trunk and moving out so they were evenly distributed to properly light the ornaments. He did it with relatively good cheer, too, considering his hands were probably all torn up by the barbs on the branches.

They all drank hot chocolate and sang Christmas carols (some in good faith, some just jokingly).

Two of the younger residents played with my toddler and had a blast. One of the older and taller residents hung some ornaments up high for me. I wasn't risking another trip to the ophthalmologist. My sons, Landon and Kellen, jumped and danced with excitement over each ornament they unwrapped and hung. Ty just smiled, knowing how important this evening was to me. And Mr. Heston, our resident wise man on loan from God and a Whetstone volunteer since its beginning, shared how meaningful the night was to him.

The evening stands at the top of the happy memory list during my time as a house mom.

A few days later, with the Christmas countdown in full swing, my beautiful Christmas tree came crashing to the ground. I don't know how it happened, since no one was around at the time. It just fell.

I dashed from the kitchen, where I was cooking, into the living room.

Glass ornaments, very special ones, our family favorites, lay scattered across the floor, some of them still spinning on the hardwood.

I was shattered. Surrounded by glass once again.

I slumped against the wall and stared at the mess. I wanted it to stay on the ground. I didn't want to pick it up. I felt like my heart had been ripped open, and setting the tree back up wouldn't fix that.

It felt deeply meaningful. Christmas, after all, is a time for symbolism.

But as I reflected on the disaster, I slowly realized I could give it new meaning. If we expected our boys to reframe the bad things that happened to them, if Whetstone had to reframe after the tornado, I could certainly do the same with a few smashed-up Christmas ornaments.

So I sat up straight. I took a few deep breaths. I closed my eyes and listened. Dinner prep could wait.

I don't want to say that Jesus *spoke* to me in that moment because I didn't hear a voice from heaven. But I did experience a peace that came from outside myself.

I remembered that even the wind and waves obey His will.

He was in control, and if he was okay with my beautiful *Southern Living* Christmas being knocked down, then I was okay with it.

Let go, Michelle.

The apostle Paul urges us to be living sacrifices. We don't have to be, I guess. But if on Christmas we don't follow in the footsteps of Jesus who gave up his seat at the right hand of God, who emptied himself and became nothing for our sake, aren't we missing out on the life-altering nature of what it means to follow God?

Later that evening, the boys lifted up the fallen Christmas tree. Everyone helped to sweep up the glass and restore the salvageable ornaments to their proper place—an honored place since they were now survivors. Gentle hands tucked back in strands of lights.

Other hands stabilized the base and readjusted the bolts.

Before dinner, we gathered in the living room to celebrate a Level Two ceremony for a boy who had finally made it past the first stage of his Whetstone journey. It's an accomplishment that cannot be achieved without surrender, letting go, and giving in. The afternoon rite symbolized the young man's progress towards honesty and self-control—the two traits we emphasize during a boy's first few months in our home, ranch, and school.

So from now on during the month of December, I'm going to celebrate my own growth towards these things as well. I'm going to look for and take time to appreciate the stars that shine out from the dark night sky.

They are not at all what I expected, but I'm learning to expect that kind of thing from God.

Chapter 45

TIME

Matt

It is a good thing for an uneducated man to read books of quotations.
—Winston S. Churchill

In my office sits a little black book I've written in throughout the years. It contains a wealth of wise sayings and super awesome quotations. (People who use the phrase "super awesome" have great need for such a thing.) It includes a broad range of authors, poets, theologians, and ancient philosophers.

In a similar spirit, Axel's schoolroom is trimmed with vintage *Time Magazine* covers accompanied by quotes from great men and women of history. From Marian Anderson to Thelonious Monk, and from Charlie Brown to Pablo Picasso. It's a halo of wisdom above the boys' desks, a cloud of witnesses that encourages them to throw off everything that hinders.

These magazines were thankfully undamaged by the tornado and thus waiting with the same sage advice as when the boys left on that dark night back in April.

For example, a boy might look up from his desk at some point during his school day and be reminded by Ernest Hemingway that "man is not made for defeat. He can be destroyed, but not defeated." The truth is up there, anchored by thumbtacks to the wall.

But the quotes are, for all their glory, without context. This particular Hemingway quote is missing the entire backstory of *The Old Man and the Sea,* although the magazine's beautiful backdrop of a giant marlin does pay homage to the short novel.

There's no questioning the value of context.

I can mangle and manipulate anything you might say into something that I want it to say. Some of our guys are experts at fabricating (or completely ignoring) context. They use it in a misguided attempt to control a reality spinning dangerously out of control. But to no avail. Trying to apply the emergency brake, they hit the gas instead. Everything comes off the tracks.

Most of life's great struggles relate to existing out of context. It's Job questioning God. Or the twentieth century experiment to make meaning for ourselves. "Hell is other people," observed the existential playwright and philosopher, Jean Paul Sartre. Life with no fixed point of reference is all dread, nausea, and angst.

In reality, suffering is reduced when it is shared—made less heavy by looking at life in light of context.

Context does not diminish or ignore. It elevates. There's a truth to the Hemingway quote without context, but when you've read Hemingway's novel, you understand it differently. You've felt Santiago's struggle. You've wrestled the fish, the expectations, the failure, the sea. With raw hands and exposed flesh, you turn pages and join in the universal struggle between life and death, destruction and defeat. So when your eyes at last run across the famous line, you have made room in your soul.

We hope it's the same for the young man who sits beneath the red-bordered *Time* pictures that adorn the schoolroom. We hope he comes to know more than facts while he studies history. We hope he discovers truth and connects to it in a way he never knew existed. That in turn he can reconnect with his parents, his family. That he can match his story to theirs and understand generational patterns within their true context. String stories forward and together.

His life, which seemed so estranged from theirs, now has a frame and a less dizzying point of view. Such a boy is not "put in his place," but "put back in his true place."

Elevated.
Contextualized.

For now we see through a glass, darkly; but then face to face: now I know in part; but then shall I know even as also I am known.
—I Corinthians 13:12

The hand of the Lord was on me, and he brought me out by the Spirit of the Lord and set me in the middle of a valley; it was full of bones. He led me back and forth among them, and I saw a great many bones on the floor of the valley, bones that were very dry. He asked me, "Son of man, can these bones live?" I said, "Sovereign Lord, you alone know."
—Ezekiel 37:1-3

Chapter 46

Dry Bones

Axel

During that first month after the tornado, Whetstone staff and supporters trudged among the bones... wondering how these bones could be made to move. We wondered if *we* could move them, or if we'd have to hire someone else with bigger, louder, and more expensive equipment to move them.

Knotty trunks the diameter of small cars don't go anywhere on their own, and if they *can* be coaxed into moving, they don't do it quickly.

So we lived with the reminders of our desolation. We spoke to them, yes, but in psalms of cursing and lament.

We used the kind of words that put the Gospel story into street terms. You know the ones—the kind that can't be misunderstood. The kind you don't necessarily put into a book you're going to publish.

In the damaged house, we got used to water stains and drywall dust and damp smells coming from behind walls and beneath carpets. The piano stood sentry beside the front entrance, waiting its turn to burn, and it became like your friendly Walmart greeter, the white and black keys forming a toothy grin that said, "Welcome. Good luck wandering the aisles trying to find whatever it is you might need today." It was in no hurry.

EVEN THE WIND – COMFORT

If the tornado wreckage held us captive, some of us succumbed to Stockholm Syndrome, falling in love with the chaos that had become our kidnapper. Why would anyone want to leave the comfort of an easy excuse?

For others, glass and rocks and stumps and nails and wires and fencing and tools and garbage became landmarks—because some point of reference is better than living in a wasteland.

Maybe this is what God thought when He took that stroll with Ezekiel among the bones. After taking a closer look at the mess, He decided a little pep talk was in order. "Do something!" he said. "Don't just sit there, wallowing in the misery of your circumstance. Try something. Try anything. Something crazy even, like talking to bones."

I think anyone watching old Ezekiel from a distance must have thought, "The old man has finally lost his mind. He's talking to dead people."

And it's interesting too that God didn't speak to the bones, which would be the logical thing. He had Ezekiel do his talking for him.

> *Then he said to me, "Prophesy to these bones and say to them, 'Dry bones, hear the word of the Lord! This is what the Sovereign Lord says to these bones: I will make breath enter you, and you will come to life. I will attach tendons to you and make flesh come upon you and cover you with skin; I will put breath in you, and you will come to life. Then you will know that I am the Lord.'"*

God could have spoken to the bones in the presence of Ezekiel, perhaps saved him a little embarrassment. He spoke the universe into existence. What are a few dry bones?

But He didn't, and that begs the question, "Why?" There must have been something important about Ezekiel prophesying to the bones.

And as I continued walking among the Whetstone bones, I suddenly remembered Moses. God had asked Moses to speak to a rock, but he had struck it with his staff instead.

"Must we bring forth water from this rock?" he said, before

his public display of righteous anger.

Beyond the obvious hubris involved with the royal "we," I think Moses missed the symbolic significance. The rock, like the bones, represented Israel. God did not want to strike his people like the cruel taskmasters of Egypt or Babylon.

He wanted to speak to them. He was saying, "Sit still and listen. Let my spirit raise you up. Know that you are dead bones without my Word."

But if God's thinly disguised metaphors escape us on most occasions, we're in good company. Moses. The apostles. The nation of Israel.

But Ezekiel, that guy got it right. He spoke to the bones.

Chapter 47

SLIDE SHOW

Michelle

It is New Year's Eve, and we are all huddled around the projector screen in the basement. All the staff and their families . . . and the Whetstone boys, of course. We're back up to five now. That's the number of boys who took shelter in this same basement nine months ago. It's family night at Whetstone Boys Ranch.

I didn't cry during the dinner beforehand. I love seeing everyone and sampling the piles of food. I enjoy watching my kids run around with all the other ranch staff kids, the number of which keeps growing. It makes me feel good to see the Whetstone boys playing games outside or sitting by the fire. I relish spending time with all the other wives and talking with dear friends.

We pray, we eat, we laugh.

Sometimes I feel a bit frazzled before large ranch gatherings, since cooking and planning for fifty people is no small task. Sometimes I don't seem to mind at all.

But if Axel has a slideshow planned, I plan on crying.

I've taken very few pictures since we moved here. Sure, I have some quick iPhone shots, which mostly amount to blurry faces of my kids and awkward poses with boys who don't really want to smile. I can't find my charger for our nice camera.

But Axel takes great pictures. Pictures of my life. I don't have to take the picture or be in the picture for it to feel like my life. The ranch is my life right now.

Tonight, the slideshow spans the entire tornado-tinged year.

My baby isn't a baby anymore. There are pictures of boys who have left our house too soon. There are pictures of boys I miss, boys I don't, and boys I kind of wish I did. Many pictures of the tornado scroll by, capturing both devastation and restoration. I watch as the roof gets blown off and then gets put back on, as trees fall down and new ones are planted, as old boys leave and new boys arrive. For thirty minutes, I watch one crazy year of my life float by.

Time is passing, and we are moving farther away from Good Friday and closer to Resurrection Sunday.

But it's good to honor the pain. It's good to reflect, to remember, to see pictures that trigger all kinds of conflicting emotion: sadness and joy mingling together. And tonight as I scan the room lit by the glow of the large moving pictures, I let both kinds of tears flow freely.

Chapter 48

YELLOW

Matt

I just drove past a posse of bright yellow Service Master trucks. It's been many months since we needed their disaster and recovery assistance, and they have moved on to serve other people in crisis.

Boys have returned to our campus, and business has resumed a semblance of normality; but seeing those big yellow trucks doesn't exactly bring back warm fuzzies. Truth be told, it wasn't their fault that the giant fans and fancy machines they set up and monitored couldn't dehumidify the outdoors. How do you dry out a house that has a huge hole in the roof and no windows? You certainly aren't going to get it done with people walking in and out of six different doors every five minutes.

I can still the hear the sound of Visqueen being sucked in and blown out every time someone dared to enter or leave. It kind of reminded me of that scene in *E.T.* where they quarantine the home with those creepy tunnel things. Imagine trying to sneak past those faceless scientists, and you'll know how I felt every time I had to retrieve a file or use the fax machine.

There was really no way the Service Master team could do their job because we were trying to do ours. We needed to move, and they needed us to stay still.

Regardless of how diligently we boarded and sealed each

window or tarped every holey section of roof, the house never functioned the way we needed it to. Quick fixes are necessary for survival, but they don't do much in the long term. The band-aid falls off, and all those triaged problems must be faced eventually. "If you don't have time to do it right," John Wooden asked his players, "when will you have time to do it over?" The yellow trucks, now in my rearview mirror, remind me of this.

Arriving at the ranch, I see that professional landscapers are finally beginning the beautification stage. It's about time. There really is no point in having a brick walkway that leads to a large concrete slab in the middle of our front lawn. It made more sense when there was a garage there.

The campus still looks ghostly at times. Disfigured trees whose limbs sprawl in all directions stand sentry, guardians to a campus that still bears the marks of a tornado. When it rains, pond-sized puddles collect in depressions of a gravel parking lot that badly needs regrading. Cavernous holes left by once majestic walnut trees continue to dot the campus. Closer to the porch, I skirt by the skeletal remains of what appears to have been a small gazebo whose remaining shingles form a grimace, and near the front steps, I cringe to see a kitschy statuette of two loving frogs seated on a bench—of all the things that a tornado would spare!

You're never supposed to judge a book by its cover, but it would be hard for anyone to avoid making some negative assumptions at this point. It's natural to question the competence of an establishment that hasn't made curbside appeal a priority.

I guess trauma tends to work like that. It barges in, breaks stuff, steals things, forces you to invent a new way to live and then mocks you for failing to clean up the mess that *it* made.

How you navigate that aftermath is no small ordeal. There is no blueprint, no map to get you through the journey. Truth be told, most of us trauma survivors are still somewhere on that journey.

Random triggers, like yellow service trucks, take us back to places we thought we left behind. Still, we are grateful for a few lessons that they have taught us.

First, when trauma comes crashing in, call it what it is. I have been tempted to refer to the tornado as "our little trauma." But no. It was a big deal because there are no quantifiers or qualifies in the land of traumatic experiences. Frustrating as it may be, trauma just is. What is traumatic to you may not be to me and vice versa. Don't downplay yours because someone else's seems bigger. Believe me, it won't affect you any less.

Second, don't beat yourself up for surviving. And I'm not talking about survivor's guilt. I'm talking about the bad choices you made when you were sad, or lonely, or depressed. For some, these life-altering decisions had irrevocable consequences. Jesus' genealogy is steeped in men and women with misguided coping mechanisms. Like them, we would do things differently if we could go back, but we can't. Instead, we must try to understand our actions and begin treating ourselves with grace. The reality is that these mistakes didn't disqualify Sarah, or Tamar, or Rahab. They didn't keep David from being a "man after God's own heart." In many ways their mistakes were qualification, not disqualification.

Thankfully, most of us don't have to deal with the guilt of a capital crime. Our difficulty lies not in what we've done to survive, but in what we failed to do. We didn't bring in the landscapers quickly enough. We didn't fill in the holes, level the ground, or stop the leaking. To all of us I say that no healing is found in the continued punishment for the currently unchangeable past. We must get on with the business of getting on.

And finally, to the Service Masters of the world—the ones who help pick up the pieces—just know you've signed up for the unfair. You're going to get hit by the blunt end of our broken dreams. You'll be collateral damage in our desperate attempt to claw out of depression and find a source of blame.

But don't quit. Don't stop caring. Pull on your rubber boots, and wade through our flooded world with us.

The waters will recede someday. And life shall wander forth.

Chapter 49

SNAPSHOT

Axel

A log cabin is rich with symbolism in the United States of America. It conjures up *Little House on the Prairie* and Walden Pond. It gives us pride to know that one of our greatest presidents was born and raised in one. A log cabin represents family, humility, ingenuity, bravery, the pioneer spirit, and much, much more.

For us at Whetstone, the log cabin is taking on a different set of symbolic implications this week as we use pine logs redeemed from the rubble of a twister. As we sand and saw, nail and notch, chisel and chink, it is easy to meditate on God's mercy to us. We have been spared.

Why some and not others is a question that will always need answering on this side of eternity, but we are grateful nonetheless, and we cannot ignore the fact that an F2 tornado seemed to leapfrog over our home, saving us from catastrophe.

In case you're wondering, what we're building is no ramshackle lean-to, but a dog-trot-styled cabin complex, pieced together with half-ton, sixteen-foot logs. Rustic, yes. Capable of being blown down with a huff and a puff? I think not. This is a house built on poured concrete, the modern equivalent of Jesus's parable in Matthew 7. Tucked away on a quiet hill and nestled in a grove of full-bodied walnut trees that look exactly like the ones blown during the tornado, the cabin will stand as a testament to faith and deliverance for decades to come.

Today the cool, sunny weather smiles down upon an extended family that has weathered the storm. We have arrived quite unexpectedly in a new world where the joy of raising things up is beginning to replace the sadness of watching things fall down.

The boys, for their part, have joined willingly in this celebration of effort. Without complaint they have moved like grown men between the difficult tasks of debarking, concrete mixing, and nail-driving. They have fought the blisters and bruises that come with exhausting manual labor.

And now, at the end of a long but rewarding week, I announce that it's time for a group picture. We have delayed the inevitable long enough. We tidy up to make the setting more presentable, winding up long orange extension cords and corralling mustard yellow concrete bags. A group congregates at the base. The younger and more adventurous climb on top of our stack of giant sticks that now stands a sturdy eight feet. There are no windows or doors. No roof. It's a strong beginning but still, just a beginning.

From my position on top of my truck cab, I tell the people on the ends to squeeze in to the center. Matt, Michelle, Jeremy, Brandon, our spouses, all of our kids, the boys. I zoom in a bit to crop out a generator and table saw. I set the timer to 10 seconds, press the button, and jump off the truck, nearly toppling the camera which rests precariously atop the tripod.

I sprint the distance between camera and cabin, scramble up the round, unchinked gaps of a few logs and spin around right before it clicks.

"Let's try a few more," I say, bouncing back to the camera before people start wandering off.

I want to get this one just right.

Even the Wind

Storms they've seen before, it isn't that,
and squalls are not uncommon.
So when the winds and waves come up,
none fear the murky bottom.

They know how ropes and sails should work
to battle nasty weather
and fight the driving rain and dark,
with knowing hands, together.

But still they sink in spite of skill,
cry out at last resort,
seek Yeshua, asleep below—
await His famed retort:

"O ye of little faith!" He speaks
rebuke to last an age,
then turning towards the gale,
"Be still!" He calms the rage.

Be still ambition, knowledge, pride,
all that beneath doth lurk;
and turn to Him who calms the seas—
the wind will do His work!

ABOUT THE AUTHOR

Matt Foster

Matt (LMFT, CTT) is the founder of Whetstone's counseling center, serving as its program director and lead therapist for seven years. He is professionally trained and certified to lead young men and their families through struggles with trauma, addiction, and attachment. He is a licensed Marriage and Family Therapist whose background includes fifteen years of experience with techniques as varied as EMDR, high ropes, outdoor/adventure, and canine therapy.

Photo courtesy of Axel Liimatta

ABOUT THE AUTHOR

Michelle Lewis

Michelle (B.A.Com.) served as Whetstone's house mom for three years. During this time, she mothered twenty-five ranch boys alongside three of her own. She is trained in Therapeutic Crisis Intervention. Today, she and her husband run a family ranch a few miles from Whetstone, where they homeschool their kids and raise sheep, cows, and Australian Shepherds.

Photo courtesy of Jessalyn Strick

About the Author

Axel Liimatta

Axel (M.Ed., NBCT) is a co-founder of Whetstone Boys Ranch and Therapeutic Boarding School, which has served nearly 100 families since 2011. He is a twenty-five-year veteran of the teaching profession, working in a wide variety of public and private school settings. He has a master's degree in secondary education, an endorsement in gifted and talented education, and certificates to teach English, Social Studies, Speech, Debate, and Theatre in grades 6–12. He earned his National Board Certification in 2007.

Photo courtesy of Boone Harding

Dear Reader,

We hope and pray that this book has been helpful to you—that Whetstone's trials and triumphs will be an encouragement in your walk with God. No two paths are the same, but there are certain valleys and vistas that resemble one another.

Perhaps our roads will cross someday, and we will share an adventure together. But if for any reason you want to take the first step, visit whetstoneboysranch.com,

    write to:

    Whetstone Boys Ranch
    6850 CR 2660
    Mountain View, MO 65548,

    call our office at 417-934-1112,

    email aliimatta@whetstoneboysranch.com,

    or check us out on Facebook, Instagram, and LinkedIn. If you like what you see, please share it with others. You never know where the wind will take it.

                          Sincerely,

                          Whetstone Boys Ranch

Use your phone's camera or QR reader to visit our website.